To Pray Is to Live

BY William P. Barker

Everyone in the Bible
When God Says No
To Pray Is to Live

To Pray Is to Live

WILLIAM P. BARKER

Fleming H. Revell Company
Old Tappan, New Jersey

Library of Congress Cataloging in Publication Data

Barker, William Pierson.
    To pray is to live.

    1. Prayer. I. Title.
BV210.2.B298   248'.3   76–54315
ISBN 0–8007–0836–9

TO
Sandy

Contents

Preface

Everything we do, including writing books, happens because of many, many others. This book on praying comes to pass because of the countless number of persons who have influenced my life for a half century, including my parents and family, and hundreds in the household of faith, Christ's church.

I must give a special word of appreciation to several persons who helped me in preparing this book. Mrs. Edward A. Whetford graciously and carefully typed the manuscript. The Reverends Susan Andrews, Gorman Roof, Brooks Smith and John Stoner, beloved colleagues at First Presbyterian Church of Allentown, offered their usual meaningful support and suggestions. Jean, my wife, Fred M. Rogers, and the Luxor Ministerial Association encouraged me to write these chapters. The Reverend and Mrs. John B. Barker and Ellen Barker provided many ideas. I am continually aware that all of these surround me with their prayer and have my deepest thanks.

WILLIAM P. BARKER

To
Pray
Is to
Live

1-The Purpose of Praying

"I want no part of your simpering piety. Praying may be fine for you, but it's meaningless to me. Prayer is empty. It feels phony to me. I believe in God, sort of, but I can't stand that prayer group stuff. Why should I pray, anyhow?"

Susan paused for breath, a bit surprised at her outburst. Jeff, her husband, looked pleased that she had been so candid. He nodded in agreement.

Susan and Jeff speak for many, even those in our churches. They are in the toddler stage of Christian growth. Turned off by the poor examples and the meager knowledge of praying they've encountered, they ask frankly, 'Why pray?'

Let's admit that they do have a point—of sorts. There has been a lot of prayer talk going around during the past few years; some of it has even driven people *from* praying! "Deliver us, O Lord, from silly devotions," salty St. Teresa of Avila once prayed. Susan and Jeff never heard of St. Teresa of Avila, but they wonder why they should pray if prayer means *silly devotions.*

Captain James Cook, the brilliant Yorkshire naviga-

tor who charted the Pacific during his epic voyages in
H.M.S. *Endeavor* was another who recoiled from *silly
devotions.* Cook even went so far as to forbid his crew
to pray, especially when the ship was in danger—which
it often was. Cook feared that prayer would rob his men
of the will to work.

Susan and Jeff, St. Teresa of Avila, Captain Cook, and
perhaps you, too, are disgusted with *silly devotions.* If
you, like Susan and Jeff, bluntly ask why you should play
games with praying the *silly devotions,* the answer is
you shouldn't. You should not be encouraged to do silly
praying.

Let's label a few of the better-known forms of silly
prayers. For the record, let's remind ourselves that
there is no reason why we should feel constrained to
pray these kinds of prayers.

Silly Prayers

1. *Touch of Etiquette.* This occurs when prayer
becomes a frill, an extra, or a polite touch.

The philosopher, Voltaire, prided himself on being
an agnostic. One day in the streets of Paris, a religious
procession passed and Voltaire reverently raised his
hat. A friend, surprised at this unexpected show of respect, asked, "Are you reconciled with God?" Voltaire
replied, "We salute but do not speak."

Prayer for some becomes such a gesture. But empty
ritual becomes a pose. Jesus denounces such playacting
as hypocrisy.

2. *Emergency Measure.* This kind of silly prayer reduces praying to a last-ditch effort to bail yourself out of a bad situation.

The father of a seriously ill youngster looked at his daughter and remarked to the pastor, "If she gets much worse, we're going to have to rely on God." Poor man, he forgot that he had always relied on God. For this father, prayer was a gimmick.

God resists our efforts to use Him, especially when prayer becomes an effort to get what we want.

3. *Chitchat.* Praying for some sinks to the level of idle gossip over the coffee cups with a heavy concern for relatively unimportant matters.

For example, one person described how he had agonized on his knees to decide whether to paint a room green or blue. Another reported that prayer meant anxiously beseeching the Lord for help in deciding whether to serve beans or peas for dinner. In a certain prayer group, two women spent considerable time petitioning God on behalf of the characters in the soap opera serial they avidly followed each day.

Although God is interested in all that we do and think, He intends our praying to rise above that absorbed with trivia. Furthermore, the breeziness in some contemporary published prayers reduces the Lord to a chum.

4. *Head Trip.* Another form of silly praying makes prayer into a heavy, throat-clearing intellectual exercise. True, we are to love the Lord God with all our minds, but we are not to twist praying into a Ph.D.

course in the philosophy of religion.

The famous French scientist-philosopher, Blaise Pascal, realized how easily he could turn his prayers into cerebral musings. For the last eight years of his life, he constantly carried a piece of parchment which reminded him that "The God of Christians is not a God who is simply the author of mathematical truths, or of the order of the elements . . . but the God of Abraham, the God of Isaac, the God of Jacob, the God of Christians, is a God of love and consolation. . . ."

Etiquette, Emergency Measure, Chitchat, Head Trip —these are a few forms of *silly devotions.* There is no reason why you should pray in any of these forms. Why then should you pray?

Born to Soar

Just because praying can degenerate into a touch of etiquette, chitchat, or head trip does not mean we may excuse ourselves from praying. Too many of us have rationalized that praying always ends as *silly devotions* —and have quit.

Many of us have willingly given up praying on a regular, sustained basis, claiming that we've not missed anything. However, we are actually like the great soaring bird in the fable who spied a piece of sweet food, and asked how he could get it.

"Give me one of your feathers," was the reply. The bird plucked a feather from a wing, and received the sugary tidbit. After all, he reasoned, what was the loss of one feather? Later, he wanted another taste of the sweet pastry. Again, he was told that it would cost him a feather. The bird, figuring he had an ample number of feathers, gladly traded another. He still flew as gracefully as before. He continued to give feathers in return for sweets, and began to discover that he could not soar as effortlessly as before. The supply, however, seemed sufficient. He exchanged more. Finally, one day, he discovered that he could no longer fly.

We have traded praying for various blandishments—and finally have discovered we can no longer rise to soar to the heights we sense we were meant to know. Recently, we have seen those who have exchanged praying for cults. We have known those who have left prayer for causes, telling themselves that picketing, not praying, gets results. We also have begun to notice how many of these as well as ourselves have become like the foolish bird, crippled, helpless, and unable to rise to what God intends us to be.

We stop praying at our own peril. We cannot live without praying any better than we can exist without breathing. To pray is to live! And to live is to pray. Life without prayer is life without God. Life without God is a nonlife.

Why pray? We pray, simply because we must have a relationship with God. "Give me thine own self, without whom though Thou shouldst give me all that Thou hast made, yet could not my desires be satisfied,"

Augustine prayed. Men and women from the Bible days knew that our lives must be grounded in God. "It is too small and unsatisfactory, whatsoever Thou bestowest on me, apart from Thyself," Thomas à Kempis reflected.

Why pray? Jesus never argues the point. He does not try to prove the need. He assumes praying is indispensable, that praying is living with the Father. Others, catching some of His insight, can say humbly, as Henry James once did, "After all, man knows mighty little, and may some day learn enough of his own ignorance to fall down and pray."

Praying keeps realigning us with God in our consciousness. Praying shoves self out of the center and puts God where He belongs. When God is at the center, we are most alive to Him, to others and to ourselves.

Lost and Found

Little William Barnett was only nine years old when he was seized and carried away by marauding Indians in central Pennsylvania in 1757. His father, horribly wounded, was scalped and left for dead. Miraculously, the father survived, although his head was terribly scarred from scalping and one arm was permanently crippled. Barnett immediately began to plan to find his son. Neighbors told him it was impossible. The boy probably had been tortured, murdered, and his small body devoured by forest animals and birds, they said.

Even if he had survived, they insisted, the youngster would have been traded to a distant tribe and raised as a brave. "Forget the boy," the other settlers advised Barnett.

Barnett, however, refused to forget young William. Patiently, at great personal risk and hardship, he searched out roving bands of Indians. At each encounter, Barnett asked to see the boys who were the age of his William. Barnett peered intently into the face of each nine-year-old.

Years passed. Barnett persisted in what everyone dismissed as folly. Traveling throughout the Pennsylvania frontier, Barnett went through the same routine of requesting permission to examine the braves who were his son's age. Occasionally, if he thought he detected a likeness to his own boy, Barnett whispered, "William! William!" His calls were always met with blank stares of incomprehension. Barnett was dismissed as a hopeless crank.

One day, seven years after William had last been seen, Barnett picked up a rumor that a white youngster had been reported living with a wandering troop of Indians. Barnett set off at once. He arrived late at night. Ushered to the place where a fair-skinned sixteen-year-old dressed in Indian garb lay sleeping, Barnett called gently, "William, William! It is your father."

The young man turned and opened his eyes. Some distant chord of memory was stirred, and he haltingly framed the word *Father.* William Barnett was found.

Praying is responding to the searching Father. Before you think of praying, He is thinking of you. Before you awoke this morning, He was awake and calling you. Long after you fall asleep this night, He will watch you. Even after you lie down for that final sleep, called death, He will remember you. He seeks you.

"In prayer," Karl Barth, the Swiss theologian, tells us, "God invites us to live with Him." It isn't enough for God to be with us in general or in the abstract. God's love is concretized in Jesus Christ. *Immanuel*—God with us! Prayer is confirmation of His being with us. We can use Gorky's words about Tolstoy to describe what Jesus Christ means to us: "I am not an orphan on earth so long as this man lives on it."

Praying means knowing that God takes us seriously. Praying means understanding that God has found us.

Most of us have been carried away by concerns other than God. Instead of taking God most seriously, we take other matters or things most seriously. Perhaps it is pleasure or hobbies or work that captures us. Sometimes it is a role or profession. Abducted by other interests, we try to forget our rightful place before God. We tell ourselves that the real world is in the culture around us, yet we secretly feel like aliens. We sense we never quite belong. We try to cover loneliness and emptiness by adopting more of the customs and cover of our strange home. Like young William in his Indian environment, however, we can never quite erase the haunting memory of an earlier relationship. We cannot forget the Father. We cannot shake the persisting re-membrance that we were meant to be with Another. We live in the world as forlorn orphans.

"I will not leave you desolate," Jesus promised (John 14:18). (Significantly, the Greek word for desolate is *orphanoi*. We can literally translate this verse, "I will not leave you orphans.") In the person of Jesus, God has come to all of us lost spiritual Williams. He calls us by name. He constantly asks us to renew the relationship which He intended for us before we were even born.

Praying is shaking off the drowsy sleep of fantasies and alienation for reality and relationship. The purpose of praying? *To be alive to God!*

Thomas Merton, lost for years in the hostile camps of hedonism and intellectualism before he finally re-sponded to the Voice calling him to a life with God, put it well. "Prayer," Merton wrote in *The Climate of Monastic Prayer*, "means yearning for the simple presence of God, for a personal understanding of His word, for knowledge of His will and or a capacity to hear and obey Him."

Why pray? Because you must take God seriously. Only when you take Him seriously can you truly take yourself seriously. And only when you take Him seriously can you take others seriously.

2-The Practice of Praying

Neighbors in Mountainside, New Jersey, were shocked and incredulous when fifteen-year-old Gregg Sanders murdered his father and mother with an axe then rushed to leap to his death from a 150-foot water tower in nearby Watchung on January 14, 1975. Gregg had been known as a bright, pleasant, likeable boy. His parents had been responsible, churchgoing people who had held the respect of everyone who knew them. It was not until after the sad funerals that police investigators were able to discover some insight into Gregg's character.

They discovered a secret room, a narrow, ten-foot long crawl space over the porch, which could be reached only through a small opening in Gregg's room. The small opening could be entered only by going on hands and knees through the kneehole of his desk. Inside the hard-to-reach, secret place over the porch, Gregg had nurtured his inner life. The boy had smuggled in an old mattress and a lamp, and had spent many hours under the eaves in complete privacy. What startled the discoverers of Gregg's hideout, however, was the astonishing collection of Nazi materials. A two-foot-wide panel with a large swastika decorated one wall. Several swastika armbands lay on the mattress. Beside the lamp was a six-page handwritten manuscript of quotations from Adolf Hitler which Gregg had carefully copied. Gregg's secret interest had been the depravity of Nazism, which he had carefully nourished in his secret room. Apparently, Hitler had become Gregg's authority to the point where Hitler's murderous ways were exhibited in the boy's behavior.

What is the nature of your inner life? You, like everyone else, have a secret place in your life where no others may enter, and where your real interests and commitments are nurtured.

The Secret Room You

That secret life actually determines who you are. "Tell me to what you pay attention and I will tell you who you are," advised the Spanish thinker Ortega y Gasset.

What is prayer? Praying begins with *being*, not with doing.

Invariably, when you think of prayer, you think of techniques. You want to hear about clever gimmicks. You are interested in shortcuts. You find yourself hung up on the gadgetry.

Often, you talk as if God is a mechanism, and prayer is a hidden switch you have to find. All this makes prayer a human activity. Praying becomes merely another skill which you think you can learn to master, like golf or bowling. Praying is reduced to another human phenomenon which can be discussed, measured, and improved. You might have noticed that most books on prayer end up as endorsements for prayer, full of surefire methods which make prayer pay off in personal success and satisfaction.

Prayer is not a stratagem. God is not a favor-granting device to be switched on by prayer. You do not find God.

Instead, God finds you. And He finds you when you face up to who you are in your secret room.

The word *hypocrite* in Greek means simply an actor, one who plays a part and wears a mask. Jesus uses the term to describe the fake, the person who is putting on an act. His stinging comments make it clear that the person trying to deceive the Lord, or others, or himself, or herself, cannot realize an authentic relationship with God.

What is behind your mask? Who is the personality in your secret life? What are your fantasies and private considerations? Who is the person in your secret room existence?

As Marcus Aurelius observed, "The soul is dyed the color of its leisure thoughts." Your secret existence ultimately determines your life. Long before the era of psychological insight, the biblical writer shrewdly noted that as a person "thinketh in his heart, so is he" (Proverbs 23:7 KJV).

Only when you forsake your con games with God, with others, and with yourself does God introduce Himself. You must admit your separation, your nakedness, your need. God will have little to say as long as you persist in deceiving Him, deceiving others about yourself, and deceiving yourself.

There comes a time when you must unmask, where the real you must stand exposed. Your playacting may be convincing to others and even to yourself. There can be no authentic relationship with anyone—with God, others, or yourself—until the authentic you is recognized.

The real you is where we start in our discussion of the *how* of praying. Being comes before doing.

Your own true being is discovered only as you know that God knows you. You have no real identity except in God. You have no genuine reality except in God. You have no authenticity except in Him. God is the reason and the fulfillment of your existence. The British theologian, Nathaniel Micklem, improving on Descartes, said simply, "I pray; therefore, I am."

As you pray, so you will *be.* You become the way you are by the way you live before God. What is your attitude toward God? This is primary in starting to pray. Don't worry about the systems and techniques of praying such as what words to use or whether to kneel, sit, or stand; these are secondary matters. Start by asking about your outlook toward God. Do you sincerely have a frame of mind in which your entire life depends on God? Do you really want to live in complete obedience before God?

Prayer as Relationship

Prayer, therefore, is communion, not conversation. Praying means relationship, not remarks. "What did you pray for?" a novice in praying asked the old Scottish lady. "Och," replied the woman, knowledgeable in the lessons of praying. "I'm passed that—just asking for things. I have taken the lid off my soul!" Praying is relating to the Lord who through Jesus Christ has chosen to relate to us.

When you "take the lid off your soul," and make your secret room existence a relationship with the One, the real you is bestowed. You are given your identity and your purpose as you realize your utter and total dependence on God, and relate to Him and to others. Forget about the pop psychology of ego-consciousness. Don't waste time on introverted quests for self-understanding. Without God, all these programs and panaceas to find yourself are dead-end streets. They enshrine your ego. Ultimately, slogans such as "Express yourself" put such weight on the self that you are unable to stand the burden. God, not self, must be at the center of your private universe as well the focus of your secret room existence.

Who Is the Other in the Relationship?

*Wait a minute. You're telling me that prayer is a
relationship with God. But that's so vague, so imper-
sonal. It's like telling me I have a relationship with the
Internal Revenue Service, or something as equally face-
less.*

Your thoughts of God may well be ill-formed and
uninformed. You may regard God as the two little girls
in the museum who came across a huge portrait of
Queen Victoria. The youngsters studied the picture
which showed the monarch in a stiff, formal pose. Finally, one girl whispered to the other, "What's she doing?" "Nothing," replied the first; "she's just reigning."
You may have the same notion of God: aloof, silent,
withdrawn; a flat, one-dimensional memory from the
past. You ask impatiently, *Who wants to relate to such
a distant, do-nothing deity?*

Start with Jesus. You probably have tried to start with
God, then have tried to figure out who Jesus is. It works
exactly the other way. When you start with Jesus, you
will be able to understand who God is.

Much of your confusion stems from trying to specu-
late on the nature of God. Ultimately, your thoughts
about God will end up in the blind alleys of conjecture.
You may have some weighty notions *about* God, but
you will not *know* God.

You know another person only as that other person
decides to disclose who he or she is. For example, you

may know all about Susan or Jeff—size, age, background, attainments, interests, hobbies, job, address, family, and schedule—but you still will not know Susan or Jeff. Knowing *about* Susan or Jeff is not enough. Only as Susan or Jeff reveal who they really are to you will you have a firsthand knowledge of them. This is what the word *revelation* means.

The same also applies to God. Only as God reveals His personality will you know God apart from hearsay and hypothesis. And the incredible announcement is that God has chosen to disclose His very Self through the person of Jesus! God was enfleshed in human form. The Almighty introduced Himself through Jesus' life, death on a cross, and reappearance to His followers. All of God's personality traits were shown clearly through the career of Jesus.

You will know what the character of God is only as you become aware of what the character of Jesus is. "If you had known me, you would have known my Father also," Jesus states unequivocally to you. "Henceforth, you know him and have seen him" (John 14:7).

In Tennessee Williams' play *The Milk Train Doesn't Stop Here Anymore,* the main character is Flora Goforth, a vulgar, volatile ex-showgirl in her sixties who has run through six marriages and a series of affairs. Her life has been empty and frivolous. From the cute actress, Flora declines to a corrupt clown. Fingers warty with jewels, she lies ill in a mountaintop villa in Italy, greedily clutching at life. Sensing that she may not be able to seduce or buy off death, her thoughts turn to religion. In a pitch of anguish, Flora cries, "Bring God to me! . . . How do you do it, whistle, ring a bell for Him?" She even frantically tinkles the little bell on her bed table.

"If you had known me . . ." Jesus asserts to you and to me, to Susan and Jeff, to all the Flora Goforths of the world through the ages, "You would have known my Father also!"

The guesswork is done. As Jesus is, so God is! Start then, with Jesus! Understand that you are entering into a relationship with the One who has definite character traits and personality, and is not a hazy, heavenly blob. Jesus may be trusted; so may God. Jesus cares; so does God. Enter into a friendship with the God who was in Christ.

How will God be real to me? How can this relationship start? Ask! Seek! Knock! And persist in asking. The verb form in Jesus' command, "Ask, and it shall be given you," (Matthew 7:7 KJV) literally means ask and ask and ask, and keep on asking.

An ancient story from the days of the desert fathers tells how a casual young inquirer asked a wise and learned monk how he could find God. "Come with me," commanded the monk. Leading the inquirer to a stream, the aged saint ordered his questioner to submerge himself. When the other was under the water, the old monk firmly placed his hands on the head of the seeker. The younger man squirmed at being held under water, but the monk steadfastly refused to release him. Seconds later, the seeker's motions became agitated. The old hermit, with surprising tenacity, continued to hold the other below the surface. The thrashing grew frantic. Finally, with a mighty lunge, the young inquirer pushed his way above the waters and inhaled great lungfuls of air. After the gasping had subsided, the ancient saint quietly spoke, "When you want God as much as you wanted air, you shall find Him."

Your praying opens with the desire for association with God. Astonishingly, you discover that He who answers prayer has initiated your praying. God has already started the conversation. Instead of yammering about your wants, you begin to understand that praying means relationship!

RAY IS TO LIVE
...od with mel-
worries
Father
...l syn-
...ter

...] Praying

...sus gave no handy-dandy tips. Nor snappy shortcuts. Instead, He gave a model prayer.

The Lord's Prayer is the pattern for all your praying.
It answers your question, *How do I pray?* by providing
a form.

Anyone who has ever done any sewing or woodwork-
ing is familiar with the use of a pattern. The pattern
outlines the piece of work and serves as a prototype.

The Lord's Prayer is the prototype of all your praying. In this model for all praying, Jesus shows the design
of your prayers. *How do I pray?* Shape your praying
according to the pattern Jesus offers.

Our Father

Start with God. Note carefully the word which Jesus
chose for God, *Father*. *Father* is a family word. Jesus
wants you to understand that the One to whom you
pray welcomes you with loving, open arms. *Father* implies the intimacy of a caring parent.

What about the words I use in praying? Do I have to

33

use Thee and Thou and learn to address G
lifluous, high-sounding phrases?

Father suggests that you can forget your
about using the proper religious words. Our
won't allow you to get hung up on vocabulary and
tax. He does not want you to feel that you have to u
impressive sentences in Elizabethan prose. In fact, th
Father probably reacts to any starchy efforts in calling
on Him in the way Queen Victoria used to complain
about the way her prime minister, W. E. Gladstone,
never spoke simply and directly but always preten-
tiously addressed her "like a public meeting." Jesus instructs you to take up the relationship in praying by
saying simply, "Father."

Please note that the word is *Father* and not *Our
Heavenly Policeman.* The One with whom you relate
in your praying comes in love.

Residents in New Castle, Pennsylvania, a few years
ago used to receive a shock occasionally when they
tried to telephone Dial-A-Prayer at the First Presbyterian Church, and heard a gruff voice answer, "State
Police." The State Police substation number was finally
changed from OL8-5531 to OL8-5575 after so many
telephoners complained that they were trying to receive help in prayer.

Perhaps you are half afraid that the Other in our
praying will respond as a punishing official. "Our Father," however, denotes the wise yet sensitive, strong
yet tender, just yet compassionate One who chooses to
relate to you.

Note also that Jesus instructs you to begin your praying "Father," not "Hey, Daddy." There is a difference between intimacy and flippancy. The relationship is with the wise, strong, and compassionate Parent-God, not a silly or senile pappy. "Father" implies respect. When you do not look up to the One with whom you are praying, you soon lose respect. And, in losing respect, you quickly lose the relationship. No wonder so many prayers seem hollow, and you feel distant from the Other.

Who Art in Heaven

Jesus wants you to understand that the God-Parent is not an extension of yourself. God is not simply the sum total of your finer impulses. The Lord is not merely a divine spark within you. The Father is a separate personality. He exists apart from you. He has a life apart from your nice thoughts and good deeds.

Praying, therefore, is not autosuggestion. Nor is praying a conversation with your own conscience. You start genuine praying when you acknowledge that the Other is not dependent on you or your thoughts in any way, but lives and moves as an autonomous and transcendent Being.

A certain family was packing in preparation to move to another city. The night before they were to leave, the small son was overheard in his prayers saying, "Well, God, I guess this is good-bye. You see, we're moving to Houston tomorrow."

"Who art in heaven" is Jesus' way of reminding you that the One who hears our prayers is not localized. God is not in any way tied to you or your little orbit.

Furthermore, "Who art in heaven" is a reminder that God is not an adjunct to this planet or merely part of nature. In some poetry and hymns, there are references to seeing God in flowers or raindrops. God is not hemmed in by the laws of the natural order. God is involved in the processes of nature, but He is more than nature and is separate from nature. It's all right to stand on a hill and admire a lovely sunset as part of God's universe, and it's permissible to gaze at a gorgeous flower and marvel at God's design. However, you do not worship that sunset or rose as God. The Father *in heaven* is distinct and disparate from lovely skies and flowers. You pray with the One who creates and sustains the universe of which our little galaxy with its tiny planet earth is but an infinitesimal part. The Father in heaven is never limited by our thinking, never measured by our laws of nature, and never hemmed in by our concepts.

Hallowed Be Thy Name

Your name tells you a great deal about who you are. Your name helps confer your sense of personhood. If you had been seized by the Nazis and taken to a death camp in World War II, one of the things taken from you would have been your name. You would have been known only as a number tattooed on your wrist. You could imagine the importance of your name if it were taken from you. You feel annoyed when someone mispronounces your name, or makes jokes about your name. You want others to take your name seriously, because when they take your name seriously, it means they take you seriously. Your name stands for you— your reputation, your individuality, and your interests.

In praying, Jesus insists that you take seriously the Father's reputation, the Father's individuality, and the Father's interests. "Hallowed be Thy name" means holding in due regard the good name of the Father.

Jesus knows your egotism. Before you can proceed with praying, you must strain out the selfishness that is part of all of your praying. Hallowing God's name means filtering out your egotism. Instead of being preoccupied with your own good name, you must do everything possible to advance the Father's good name.

What is God's name? The early Hebrews treated the name with such reverence that they were prohibited from speaking it. Only the High Priest, on one day each year inside the Holy of Holies of the Temple, was permitted to verbalize God's name. Even today, we have only the four consonants, the Hebrew letters YHWH, for the name of God. So carefully did our spiritual ancestors guard the name that we can only guess at the way they pronounced those four consonants. (Perhaps it was pronounced Yahweh.)

Jesus sums up all that ever was contained in the name of God. He assumes the embodiment of the interests and reputation of the Father. When you pray, you do not trifle with Jesus. Prayer means taking Him seriously. Disregarding His demands is desecrating the name. Serious regard for Jesus means hallowing the Father's name.

Thy Kingdom Come

In 1776, when feeling against the English monarchy ran strong, the Bruton Parish Church in Williamsburg, Virginia changed the wording of all the prayer books from the *kingdom of God* to the *republic of God.* References to kings and kingdoms did not set well.

The word *kingdom* is used deliberately in your pattern for praying. It refers to the Father's realm, the Father's rule. And, as Lord, He is the undisputed Master. His rule is not a democracy in which He is elected by popular vote and subject to recall. He is absolute in authority.

You can pray meaningfully only when you acknowledge His complete authority. Your prayers have significance and substance only when you pray for the Father's rule to be extended.

"Thy kingdom come" bluntly says for you to pray "Your realm, O Father, be extended. *Your* realm—not mine—be extended, starting with me!"

His realm must take in your entire life. You may not

hold back anything from His rule. Otherwise, your praying will be a sham.

When the earliest missionaries converted the Frankish tribes, they sometimes baptized the chieftains and their entire armies. At first, the missionaries were puzzled when these chiefs and their followers immersed themselves completely except for their right arms, which they held above the water. These bold warriors willingly dedicated everything to Christ except their right arms. Later, the missionaries discovered that their converts continued their bloody warfare as before on the grounds that they never had their sword arms baptized. Christ's realm did not include their weapons or fighting arms.

How do I pray? Jesus insists that you recognize that His dominion includes every part of your life. Your wallet, your income, your leisure, your body—*everything* you are and possess must be placed under His control.

In addition to the private sector of your life, the Father's kingdom also includes the public. In your citizenship and in your life in the community you must live the prayer that His realm take precedence over every other realm.

The Dutch Christians during World War II knew what it meant to pray, "Thy kingdom come." When the Nazis directed these church people to refuse justice to Jews, these valiant members of the Father's realm recognized who was the ultimate ruler by rep-

lying; WE CANNOT OBEY YOU NAZIS BECAUSE
CHRIST IS LORD. YOU AND WE HAVE TO REN-
DER FINAL ACCOUNT TO HIM WHO IS FINAL
JUDGE.

Thy Will Be Done

How do I pray? The model prayer provides the pattern for your praying and urges you to seek to fulfill the
Father's will here in this world, now.

Praying changes you, not God. Its purpose is to bring
about that change. "When a seaman throws his boat
hook ashore," wrote doughty old Matthew Henry, "and
it grips, and he starts pulling on the rope, he is trying
not, poor fool, to haul Britain to the boat, but the boat
to the shore. And he does it."

This is real praying. You must will the will of God.
Forget about trying to tug God into carrying out your
whims. This showdown of wills is at the heart of every
prayer. "All who seek their own will are of the company
of the crucifiers," warns William Law in his classic, *A
Serious Call to a Devout and Holy Life.*

When your will is given over to doing the Father's
will, prepare for great things! "I am not master of myself, but obey Him who commands me to speak plain
and flatter no flesh upon the face of the earth," exclaimed Scotsman John Knox, and it is no wonder that
he altered both the character and history of his people.
And so may you!

Provision, Pardon and Protection

How do you pray? Do you badger God with a list of demands? Maybe you think of prayer as relating your gimmies.

Jesus' model prayer skips the requests until near the end. The first part deals entirely with straightening out the relationship between you and the Father. Only when you are in the proper relationship implied in the first petitions of the Lord's Prayer may you continue and bring your needs to the Father.

Astonishingly, Jesus reduces all your needs to three: (1) provision, (2) pardon, and (3) protection. Probably your prayer requests have been like the acquisitive tot who put through a long distance telephone call shortly before Christmas in 1973 to North Pole, Alaska, to ask for Santa Claus. The child was connected with the Santa Claus House Trading Post, and recited such a long list of requests, that he ran up a ninety-seven-dollar phone bill. Praying must never make the Lord into a celestial Santa.

Say We

You will notice that there is no *me, my, mine,* or *I* anywhere in the pattern for praying given by Jesus. All of the personal pronouns are first person plural (*"Our* Father . . . Give *us . . . our* daily bread; forgive *us* our debts as *we* forgive . . . Lead *us* not into temptation, but deliver *us . . ."*). Praying is always done with brothers and sisters in mind.

If you really have communion with the Father, you always have this relationship, not for your own sake, but also for the sake of others. A test for the honesty and authenticity of your praying is: How much are you aware of others?

There is a kind of counterfeit prayer which focuses on you alone and excludes others. Turned in on your own personal interests, you narrow your praying field, like the old Ohio farmer who reduced praying to:

> Bless me and my wife;
> Son John and his wife;
> Us four;
> No more.
> Amen.

Such solo praying, like solo drinking, is an invariable sign of a neurotic personality.

Our Daily Rations

You may pray for your daily needs only when you remember the two thirds of your brothers and sisters in today's world who are hungry or undernourished. Praying "Give *us . . . our* daily bread" means agreeing to pass the bread along the table to those who have none.

And you may ask only for bread, not cake with icing and cherries on the top. Jesus says "bread," the plain, ordinary, everyday stuff. You must be realistic in your praying, and ask for needs, not frills.

Forgiven and Forgiving

The more that you are united to the Father in love, the more you are united to others, because there is one love that embraces both God and your brothers and sisters. You give to others in direct proportion to what you receive from the Father. And you receive His mercy in direct proportion to the mercy you share with others. Paradoxical? Of course! Love never makes sense. The Cross defies explanation. "Forgive us . . . as we forgive," Jesus rightly instructs.

Years ago in rural Canada, a dog broke loose and mauled a two-year-old girl so severely that the child died. The dog's owner immediately destroyed the animal, and tried to call on the parents of the dead child. The youngster's parents, grim and angry, refused to permit the man to see them. The dog's owner tried every possible way to express his regrets and sympathy, and, most importantly, to beg forgiveness for the horrible act done by his dog. Locked in bitterness, the little girl's parents rebuffed every attempt of the unhappy man. The hurt began to affect both families. Meanwhile, both the dog's owner and the dead child's parents tried to keep up the pretense of religion.

One spring night, a fire broke out in a barn owned by the man who had owned the dog. The hapless man was ruined; the blaze destroyed livestock, implements, tools, and even the seed for planting. Two days later, when the man arose, he was surprised to see that someone had plowed and planted a crop during the night. Tracing the tracks, he found to his surprise that the person who had done the planting was the neighbor whose little girl had been killed by his dog. The onetime dog owner timidly knocked on the door of the home where the grieving farmer lived, and hesitantly asked if he had sown the crop for him, and why.

Quietly but firmly, the other replied, "Aye, I sowed seed in your field so God could exist."

Withhold forgiveness, and you refuse to allow God to exist. You become an atheist anytime you refuse to forgive! Forgive those who hurt you and you permit the Parent-God to be real. You know that grace which the Forgiver extends as you distribute it to others.

Delivered

The model prayer concludes with a final request—for protection.

The word *temptation* means three things in the Greek text: testing, trial, and temptation. You are praying for strength to stand fast when you sense you are being tested, or going through trying times, or feeling tempted. Satan, the personification of evil, is sometimes referred to as the tempter, showing the ever present and superhuman dimensions to temptation.

"Lead us not into temptation" does not mean that God sometimes lures you into a trap. Rather, Jesus instructs you to pray, in effect, strengthen us to stand when we are ready to give in; help us to ward off the tempter.

Snatch us from the jaws of the destructive powers is the meaning of "Deliver us from evil." Pray with the confidence that the Deliverer has come, and stands with you in your daily battle for survival. Through the Spirit, the Risen Lord gives you the protection you need as you ask!

Persist in shaping your praying on the prototype. You will discover that although you can rattle through the Lord's Prayer in eight seconds, you will never master all its meaning in your lifetime. Meanwhile, let the model given by the Master Pray-er answer your questions on the *how* of praying.

4-The Place of Praying

When do I pray? When I'm in trouble? When I feel like it? Mainly when I am at church?

Often, we are like the small boy who, when asked by his Sunday-school teacher whether he said grace at his home before eating, replied, "Naw, we don't need to pray. My Mom's a good cook."

Jesus' life was saturated with prayer. Read the Gospel accounts. Notice how frequently these mention His praying. His disciples saw Him in prayer often. They were sometimes slow-witted at understanding Jesus' words. But they swiftly grasped the secret behind His life, His praying.

Jesus was a marvelous teacher, but His followers did not say to Him, "Teach us to teach." He was a successful healer, but people did not say, "Teach us to heal." Jesus was a superb preacher, but His disciples did not ask, "Teach us to preach." Sensing the inner dynamics of His power, they begged, "Lord, teach us to pray" (Luke 11:1).

Jesus teaches us to pray with the Lord's Prayer, the model prayer which is the pattern for all praying. He also teaches us to pray with His life. Through the example of Jesus' life, we understand the place of praying in our own lives.

When You Want to Know God's Plans for You

Dag Hammarskjold, the twentieth-century seeker who died while serving as the secretary-general of the United Nations, kept a journal which was later published under the title, *Markings.* In a 1952 entry, Hammarskjold mused, "What I ask for is absurd: that life shall have a meaning. What I strive for is impossible: that my life shall acquire a meaning."

In your own way, you have asked the same question. And, in your own way, you already sense that the answer has something to do with God's plans for you. You ask, however, "How can I know those plans?"

Pray! Jesus did. At the start of His career, His baptism, He asked for confirmation of His identity and mission. Luke 3:21 specifically states that Jesus "was praying." In response to that praying, Jesus was given a call and a command. "Thou art my beloved Son; with thee I am well pleased" (Luke 3:22). The Spirit was upon Jesus, and Jesus understood that He was God's chosen one. "Thou art my beloved Son" comes from the coronation ceremony for the king (*see* Psalms 2:7), and "with thee I am well pleased" comes from the Servant Songs (Isaiah 42:1) which describes the way God's servant must suffer for others. Jesus clearly understood that

God's plans meant for Him to be the divinely anointed King or Messiah of Israel, but entailed sacrificing His life as the suffering servant. God's plans were clearly laid out in answer to Jesus' prayers.

His plans will also be laid out for you—when you persist in praying.

"I have been driven many times to my knees by the overwhelming conviction that I had nowhere else to go," stated Abraham Lincoln. "My own wisdom and that all around me seemed insufficient for the day." The martyred president, who was perhaps America's greatest nineteenth-century theologian, had discovered the place of praying in his life, particularly when it came to understanding God's plans.

When you pray to know God's plans for you, you discover that God illumines each moment with meaning. You may live every day as if it is your first! You see astonishing possibilities everywhere. God discloses significance to everything and everyone when you pray!

"Nothing of importance happened today," was the entry in King George III's diary on July 4, 1776. The person who prays little discerns little.

Are you inclined to mumble with Edna St. Vincent Millay, "Life must go on; I forget just why"? Do you wonder if God has any intentions for your life? Continue praying! You will receive insights into His plans.

A. J. Cronin, the Scottish novelist, described a middle-aged nurse named Olwen Davies who served on an inadequate salary in the village of Trogenny. Cronin asked her why she continued to live in such a forgotten place on such pitifully small pay. After all, he reminded her, she was worth much more. Nurse Davies answered quietly that it was all right because she had enough to get along. But Cronin insisted, "You ought to have a pound a week at least. God knows you're worth it!" Miss Davies paused before she slowly answered, "Doctor, if God knows I am worth it, that is all that matters to me."

God, who knows your worth, reveals His plans when you live in a prayer relationship with Him as Jesus did.

When You Are Under Pressure

Jesus was unquestionably the busiest person who ever lived. He also lived under greater pressures than anyone before or since. People badgered Him wherever He went. His schedule was filled every waking minute during His ministry. He was frequently interrupted by crises. His career required a series of major decisions. He was no dreamy-eyed recluse, shielded from the exhausting, exasperating Monday through Saturday survival march which you experience each week! Jesus went through it, too—and more so.

How did He manage? The answer is so obvious we overlook it. "He rose and went out to a lonely place, and there he prayed" (Mark 1:35) after a hectic time preaching and healing in Capernaum. "But he withdrew to the wilderness and prayed," after a physically and emotionally tiring period of serving in Galilee

(Luke 5:16). Following the interruption of His prayer retreat when the crowds came and needed to be fed, He fed them. "After he had dismissed the crowds, he went up on the mountain by himself to pray" (Matthew 14:23); "After he had taken leave of them, he went up on the mountain to pray" (Mark 6:46). Faced with furious opposition and deadly plots as He continued his ministry, "he went out to the mountain to pray; and all night he continued in prayer . . ." (Luke 6:12), then reached His decision on choosing the Twelve.

Prayer enables you to preserve your sanity when under pressure. How do you cope with tension? By medication or drugs? (Americans swallowed some 17 billion aspirin tablets last year—an average of seventy-seven per person—according to research at Duke University Medical Center, and spend approximately $280,000,-000 annually on tranquilizers. The three-martinis-before-dinner business executive says he has to unwind —and wonders why nearly 25 percent of all junior and senior high school students are heavy or moderately heavy drinkers, as a nationwide survey by Research Triangle Institute revealed.)

Perhaps you have been into meditation courses. Some with esoteric mumbo jumbo and exotic eastern terms have brought their promoters immense fortunes. Perhaps you have observed that few of these have any reference to God, but emphasize techniques for achieving some sense of calm. Eventually, as many former advocates of the transcendental meditation craze have discovered, mumbling a mantra for twenty minutes, twice a day after a $125 course is a rip-off. Long before any maharishi-imported form of meditation hit these shores, Jesus and His followers had understood the art and discipline of meditation. Let the Master, not a maharishi, be your mentor!

Prayer as relationship with God clears your mind and allows Him to energize you. Praying as contemplation helps you to back off from frustration and to find new resources in life. Jesus shows you that God-focused meditating allows the Father to help you to organize your thoughts, to reflect positively about your past and future, to decide your next line of action, to calm yourself, and to sort out your priorities. You will discover that these times of being still and knowing, of not saying but being before God, will provide you with the stamina to stand up to any pressures. The busier your schedule and the tougher your decisions, the more you must pray!

When You Eat

There are at least ten accounts in the Gospel records of Jesus praying before eating. Never were these prayers regarded as pious gestures. In every case, Jesus' prayers before meals were for thanksgiving and for sharing.

On some occasions, there was not enough food to go around. His disciples shrugged, "We have only five loaves here and two fish" (Matthew 14:17) when hungry hordes descended on them unexpectedly. Jesus took this trifling amount (perhaps a typical lunch) and prayed. In spite of apparent insufficiency, He prayed. His praying over the pitifully puny resources in the midst of hungry crowds is mentioned by Matthew, Mark, Luke, and John in their accounts of the feeding of the five thousand (the only miracle story mentioned by all four Gospel writers).

"Bread for myself is an economic problem, bread for my brother is a spiritual problem," stated Nikolai Berdyaev, the Russian philosopher. When you sit down at any meal, you never eat as the only member of God's family. The needs of your brothers and sisters are on God's mind, and must be in your prayers.

You have probably heard so much about world hunger during the past few years that you are weary and bored. Like the disciples, you feel like shrugging that you have only slender resources and ask "What are they among so many?" (John 6:9). Jesus still commands, however, "You give them something to eat!" (Matthew 14:-16).

Therefore, pray when you eat. Pray that you may be so sensitized to the goodness and nearness of Jesus Christ that you may care. Pray that you may be so sensitized to the needs of brothers and sisters that you may share. A nation with more than 71 million household dogs and cats, consuming as much food required to keep 47 million people in good health, needs to learn

to pray before eating. Pray for the 500 million in the
world who are starving. Pray for the 1,100,000 infants
and children in the U.S. who, according to a University
of California study, are suffering from undernourish-
ment severe enough to hamper their brain develop-
ment.

And pray thankfully for the miracle of enough food
for yourself. Pray also for the blessing of an appetite, a
healthy body, and the family and friends with whom
you may enjoy your meal. Never let your praying at
meal time be perfunctory. Luther's comment on praying applies to a grace at table as well as to other prayers:
"None can believe how powerful prayer is and what it
is able to effect but those who have learned it by experience!"

When Others Are Ill

Christians today tend to react to the illness of others
by lining up in one of two camps, the let-medical-
science-take-care-of-them group, or the let-God-take-
care-of-them group. Most mainline denominations, except for a highly vocal charismatic fringe, line up in the
first camp. The Pentecostals, many sect groups, and the
faith healers fall into the second.

In southwest Colorado, for example, the several-hun-
dred members of the Church of the First Born insist
upon praying instead of seeking medical help ever. In
February, 1976, a three-year-old boy died of diphtheria

THE PLACE OF PRAYING

and a year earlier his four-year-old cousin had died of the same deadly and highly contagious disease. Neither had received any immunization or treatment. Reverend John Carver, the pastor and also the grandfather of the two dead boys, explained that healing is provided by God, "not by doctors or drugs."

When you hear of such tragic and unnecessary deaths, perhaps you react in a negative way toward all prayer for the sick. Maybe you firmly reject intercessory prayer, *period*, or have such a distaste toward praying for the sick that you are like the theologian, Reinhold Niebuhr, who, when hospitalized was told by David Roberts that all of Union Theological Seminary where he served as dean, was praying for his recovery. Niebuhr protested mightily, thundering, "I want no one lobbying for me in the court of the Almighty!"

Prayer or penicillin? Is this the way you see it? With Jesus, however, it was not such an *either-or* decision. Rather, it was both. Jesus prayed for the ill. He also used standard medical procedures.

Almost side by side in Mark are two episodes which illustrate how Jesus believed in both prayer *and* penicillin. Mark 9:14–29 describes an apparently hopeless case in which a little boy is healed of his seizures by Jesus after the disciples were unable to help the youngster. When pressed by His followers why they failed, Jesus said, "This kind cannot be driven out by anything but prayer" (Mark 9:29). In the previous chapter of Mark, Jesus encounters another stubborn case, a man with an eye problem which left him blind. Jesus uses His saliva—which everyone in those days believed to have healing properties as a form of medication—as a kind of ointment on the man's eyes, and restores his sight (See Mark 8:22–26).

All this is Jesus' way of instructing you to care for others in every way. With Jesus, no person is "officially unimportant" as Robert Frost put it. Therefore, with His example and in His name, pray earnestly for those who are ill. Don't be daunted by the medical odds; your task is not to assess whether the other is worth praying for or is too far gone. There are no triage theories in praying! Pray—and leave the rest in God's capable hands.

When You Are Uncertain About Others

Sometimes the communication gap seems to be a chasm. You feel frustrated because others do not seem to understand you. "We must not die before we have explained ourselves to each other," wrote aging Thomas Jefferson to his longtime friendly adversary, John Adams. You, also, are not certain about how others hear you.

"Who do the people say that I am? . . . Who do you say that I am?" Jesus asked His friends (Luke 9:18, 20). According to Luke's account, the question stemmed from an occasion after Jesus had been praying. Jesus felt uncertain about how He was being understood, and prayed about it.

His prayers were answered when He was led to ask, "Who do you say that I am?" and Peter made the ringing reply, "The Christ of God!" (Luke 9:20). About a week later, Jesus' concerns over His disciples' comprehension of who He was were put more at ease. He took Peter, James, and John on a prayer retreat on Mt. Hermon. High on the slopes of the mountain, "as he was praying" (Luke 9:29) these three men received a vision —the Transfiguration—giving them insight into the place of Jesus in God's scheme of history. Once again, the setting was prayer.

In your confusion and apprehension about communicating with others, pray! The Holy Spirit aids your efforts to speak and hear. You are led to understand that you are not alone. As Abraham Heschel, the Jewish philosopher and theologian, once said, "I am a multitude when I pray." You become a soul brother or sister to those you feel uncertain about.

When You See Others Slipping or Failing

Have you ever watched others get deeper into trouble because of their carelessness, stupidity, or selfishness? Leon Jaworski, former special prosecutor for the Watergate investigation, described how he felt about those indicted: "Still fresh on my mind is the sadness of seeing one of the great tragedies of modern history— men who once had fame in their hands sinking to infamy—all because their goals were of the wrong dreams and aspirations. The teachings of right and

wrong had been forgotten and little evils were permitted to grow into great evils, small sins to escalate into
big sins."

This is the way Jesus felt about Peter just before the
crucifixion. The is the way you may feel about a friend,
a relative, an associate whom you see sinking morally
and spiritually. What do you do about the other? Erase
his name by ignoring him? Tell her off?

When blustery, big-mouthed Peter showed unmistakable signs of moral collapse, Jesus quietly told him,
"I have prayed for you that your faith may not fail; and
when you have turned again, strengthen your breth-
ren" (Luke 22:32). Jesus prayed for Peter! And in praying for Peter, Jesus still saw possibilities in Peter,
though he was weak and undependable.

When you pray for others when they are slipping or
failing, you begin to notice possibilities in them which
you never noticed before. Astonishingly, you also find
that others live up to the possibilities you see in them.

Gutzon Borglum, the sculptor who carved the famous bust of Lincoln, had a cleaning woman who
dusted the block of marble from which the great carv-
ing was sculpted. To the cleaning woman, the chunk of
marble was simply one of the many shapeless blocks
amidst the clutter. One day, after Borglum had started
sculpturing the block, chipping until the unmistakable
profile of Lincoln began to emerge, the cleaning
woman studied the block, then rushed to Borglum's
secretary, asking, "Ain't that Abraham Lincoln?" When

told it was, she exclaimed, "Well, how in the world did Mr. Borglum know that Lincoln was in that piece of marble?"

How did Jesus know that an apostle was in that fickle fisherman, Peter? He knew through praying. How may you know that a disciple is in that block of flesh which is your friend, who is slipping? Again, you know through praying.

When You Are Tempted

You will be tempted. Don't ever make the mistake of thinking that temptation always comes in lurid forms, such as the chance to abscond with $5 million or to run off with a Hollywood star, and, therefore, will never happen to you.

Jesus was tempted. His temptations might not have been the same as yours, but they were just as real. Your temptations will not be exactly like His, but they will be just as difficult to handle.

Revelation 9:1–10 describes temptations as huge locusts swarming like a plague, but with bodies like horses, faces like humans, hair like women, and tails like scorpions. The symbolism is obvious. Temptations, like horses, are more powerful than you. With human visages, temptations always appear rational and plausible. Temptations, like beautiful women, are attractive. But with a hidden sting like scorpions, temptations are also deadly.

As Jesus agonized with His temptations at the start of His ministry and in the Garden of Gethsemane, so you will be forced to wrestle with your temptations in prayer. Perhaps these prayers will not be well worded. Don't worry about using elegant phrases in these prayers. As John Bunyan, who knew about praying and temptations as a Baptist preacher in seventeenth-century England, once said, "The best prayers have often more groans than words." Jesus' words in His praying during times of temptation will brace your praying better than any others: "Nevertheless not my will, but thine, be done" (Luke 22:42).

When You Suffer

You will never be exempt from suffering just because you pray. Prayer is not a lucky charm.

Some suffering, of course, is the result of your own sinfulness and stupidity. You can accept that kind of suffering, because you can tell yourself that you have only yourself to blame.

But some suffering is caused by the sinfulness and stupidity of others. You are the victim. Life does not seem just. God seems blind. You must be a loser. Raised on the Vince Lombardi philosophy that "winning isn't everything; it's the only thing," you resent being made to take your lumps because of others.

The worst thing about suffering, you eventually discover, is the terrible loneliness. You feel desolate. Even

God seems helpless. Reformer John Calvin described the sense of hopelessness in real suffering when he wrote to a friend in a dark hour of his own life, "The future appalls me. I dare not think of it. Unless the Lord descends from heaven, barbarism will engulf us."

No one knew the depths of personal suffering more than Jesus. His words from the Cross, "My God, my God, why hast thou forsaken me?" (Matthew 27:46 and Mark 15:34) will always send a chilly shudder through you. You realize that He had to drain the cup of suffering, not just take sips as you and I do.

In His suffering, however, Jesus prayed. The words, "My God, my God, why hast thou forsaken me?" are actually a form of praying. The prayer has a grim, tell-it-like-it-is honesty. Like the prayers of Job and Jeremiah, who were among God's closest companions, the prayer even arraigns God.

Jesus' prayer, "My God, why . . . ?" may be a cue for starters in your praying when you suffer. God understands your aching loneliness, and you may open the conversation with Him with the bluntness and anger which you undoubtedly feel. You may ask, "Why am I suffering?" God knows, however, that you really don't require answers. You need comfort. And He has already sent the Comforter. Your most profound needs in your suffering have already been met, but you must pray. Then keep praying.

The words, "My God, my God, why hast thou forsaken me," which Jesus spoke from the Cross are actu-

ally a quotation from Psalm 22. If you read Psalm 22,
you will be struck with the similarities between what
Jesus was enduring on the Cross and what the Psalm
describes. Psalm 22 is a commentary on the agonies and
disgrace a crucified person would have experienced.
The psalm does not end, however, on a somber note of
defeat. Instead, there is a triumphant shout of praise.
The psalmist affirms, "Dominion belongs to the Lord,
and he rules over the nations" (Psalms 22:28).

Pray when you suffer. Pray honestly. Pray confi-
dently. Even in your suffering as you pray, you will be
able to express God's ultimate power and goodness, as
St. Francis de Sales did frequently in his favorite
prayer, "Yes, Father! Yes! And always Yes!"

When You Have Been Offended

Even if you could succeed in surrounding yourself
with the most pleasant and considerate religious people
in the world, you would still find that there would be
times when they would hurt you. You will never discover a Utopia filled with perfectly loving people who
will never offend you! The earth contains people like
you and me who are hopelessly flawed, and therefore
succeed in inflicting deep hurts. In short, you will be
hurt many, many times in addition to the many, many
times you have already been hurt.

Perhaps the hardest prayer you will ever have to
pray is the prayer of forgiveness. "I forgave a man

once," whispered a convict to his priest, "and it damn near killed me." You have to die to forgive—die the death of self-pride; die the death of personal dignity.

Among Jesus' last prayers was the petition from the Cross, "Father, forgive them; for they know not what they do" (Luke 23:34). Jesus' prayer for forgiveness was for the soldiers who brutally hammered the nails through His hands and feet, for the crowd who callously watched Him writhe, for the religious leaders who taunted Him, for the disciples who deserted Him, for Pilate and Herod who shirked responsibilities, for His own people who failed to respond to His call, and for all who participated in the greatest atrocity of history. Jesus *prayed* for them! Not cursed them or ignored them, but prayed!

In Lebanon, Indiana, in 1976, the son of the Reverend Ollie G. Wilson was killed by Officer Michael Slagle of the Indiana State Police when young Wilson pointed a gun at him. Mr. Wilson, a contractor and part-time pastor at the Green Street Wesleyan Church, felt the deep hurt of knowing that his son, Stan, had been shot at the scene of a robbery. Worse, Mr. Wilson also felt the hurt of the irreplaceable loss of his precious boy. Mr. Wilson prayed. Shortly afterward, he made a public plea in an advertisement in the *Lebanon Reporter.*

"I trust some way, somehow, you'll have God-felt mercy and forgiveness toward my son, Stan, to forgive his deed," the advertisement read. "And have sympathy for Officer Slagle for the badge of sorrow he feels and will wear silently and unseen and unspoken down through the rest of the years of his life. . . ."

You *must* pray in the spirit of Him who said, "Father, forgive," when He was hurt. Only then will you be given healing!

When You Lie Down to Sleep

Jesus' last words before His death on the Cross were a prayer, "Father, into thy hands I commit my spirit" (Luke 23:46). How appropriate that He closed His career as He had lived it—in praying.

The words also were the "Now I lay me down to sleep" which Jesus and all other Jewish children lisped as their earliest bedtime prayer. Possibly the first and the last prayers Jesus ever spoke were these beautiful words from Psalms 31:5. From Mary's knee until near the Father's throne, Jesus could fall off to sleep with a prayer of commitment.

When you lie down at night, pray. If you do not know how to begin a nighttime prayer, use the words of the psalm taught to Jewish youngsters, "Father, into thy hands I commit my spirit." Commit yourself into the capable and loving hands of the One who continues to keep wakeful watch beside your bed. Whether you wake or sleep, whether you remember or forget, this God knows and cares. When you cannot get to sleep, continue praying as you commit your life into His keeping. Your brain may not seem to be switched off, and the gift of sleep may not be given immediately, but you may be certain your prayers of commitment mean that He will provide enough refreshment for you to do whatever tasks He has in mind for you on the following day.

"We die as we have lived," writes Michael Roemer; "we bring to this last great act of our lives whatever we have brought to earlier acts." (*Quote*, May 16, 1976) The kind of praying we do each night carries over to the kind of praying we will do when we must face that final sleep called death.

When you must lie down for *that* sleep, do so with the same confidence as when you lie down this evening. The God who kept commitments with Jesus by raising Him up alive at Easter after the death on the Cross, will keep His commitment to you. Pray with hope, even when you must die!

5-The Parameters of Praying

Is every prayer the same? Do I have to follow a set order when I pray? Are there different kinds of prayers?

You and God conduct your own conversations in praying. No relationship has every line already written into a script, but thrives on spontaneity and variety. Your prayers, like your talk with anyone you feel close to, will assume different shapes in different circumstances.

Through the centuries, however, the community of faith has charted these different shapes which prayers may take. These parameters of praying are *Adoration, Confession, Thanksgiving, Supplication, Intercession,* and *Dedication.* No prayer, of course, must necessarily always include each of these parameters. And each parameter does not exclude the others. Each overlaps on the other: Adoration spills over into Confession, which in turn gives way to Thanksgiving, while Thanksgiving also means a movement to Adoration again. But at the same time that all six parameters are like interlocking circles, there is also a progression. Prayers move from Adoration to Dedication and back again. Each of these parameters deserves some special consideration.

Adoration

A Boston newspaper once complimented the Reverend Theodore Parker for rendering "the finest prayer ever addressed to a Boston audience." This sums up the failing of too many prayers: they are addresses to an audience instead of adoration of the Other.

There are occasions in which your praying must take an attitude of sheer wonder and praise of God for God's sake. The old New England farmer, sitting down to a sparse meal in lean times with his family, knew this when he prayed, "We thank Thee, Lord, that we have Thee and all this besides." Mother Teresa of Calcutta, the tiny nun who works among the poorest of the poor in India, is another who understands the meaning of adoration. Refusing all accolades, this contemporary saint said simply, "We have nothing. The greatness of God is that He has used this nothing to do something." Such a comment springs from an attitude of adoration of God. Have your prayers taken on the glow which stems from appreciating the Lord for His own sake? When they do, you will begin to comprehend the meaning of that quaint term, *loving the Lord*.

Probably you won't find prayers of adoration coming easily at first. You may feel a vague kinship with the country gentleman with whom the English novelist, William Somerset Maugham, once stayed. This man, Maugham observed, "was a religious man and he read the prayers to the assembled household every morning. But he had crossed out in pencil all the passages in the

Book of Common Prayer that praised God. He said there was nothing so vulgar as to praise people to their faces, and he could not believe that God was so ungentlemanly as to like it."

The more your prayer life deepens, however, the more you find yourself adoring God. You will understand why the rugged crew of English Puritans put as the first question and answer in the Westminster Catechism of 1647:

Q. What is the chief end of man?

A. Man's chief end is to glorify God and enjoy Him forever.

In the altar area of Our Lady's Church in Copenhagen, Denmark, you may see the famous statue of Christ carved by Bertel Thorwaldsen. To appreciate fully the significance of the magnificent piece of sculpture, however, you must kneel at the feet of the statue and look up into the face. Perhaps Thorwaldsen intended this as a parable. You must kneel and look up before you can adore. To understand God, you must first *stand under* Jesus Christ. This is adoration.

Confession

In E.M. Forster's *Passage to India,* the heroine leaves England to go to India to question India and life. Before she returned, however, "she was no longer examining life, but being examined by it."

You discover the same thing in your journey of life. Being examined by life, you discover things about yourselves which dismay and disappoint you.

Every person's life carries failure and a wish for what might have been. When Leonardo da Vinci painted *The Last Supper,* he had difficulty in finding models for only two of the thirteen faces in the great fresco. Finally, da Vinci found a person with a face suitable for the portrait of Christ, a young singer in the Milan cathedral choir. The face of Judas, however, went vacant for many years. The artist rejected one model after another. Finally da Vinci found the figure to pose for Judas in a prison in Rome. After he had sketched the man for several days, da Vinci was appalled to learn that the man had posed previously for him, and had been the person whom the artist had painted in *The Last Supper* as Christ.

You also will discover that your portrait can be used for both Christ and Judas. You will have to acknowledge this to God and yourself before your praying-relating will take on deeper significance. You may try to ignore or gloss over this Judas side of your life, but sooner or later you will have to deal with it.

Residents of an Ontario town paid little attention when a radium-extraction plant was torn down more than twenty years ago until the rubble and salvaged building materials used in other construction turned out to be contaminated with radiation. The detection of radioactivity in a new Toronto office building, which occurred after a photographer had complained that his film was being mysteriously fogged, led to the discovery of radiation in the town where the rubble had come from. The radiation count in some areas of the town necessitated the removal of six families and an expensive cleanup operation, although the deadly contamination had occurred more than twenty years earlier.

Guilt is a deadly contamination in your life. Eventually, you must dispose of it. Even though you may tear down its cause, its effects will linger for years. You must clear away guilt although you have tried not to notice it. Otherwise, guilt's damaging effects will continue and ultimately destroy.

Prayers of confession are necessities, not options, in your life. Don't gag on confessing your sin. From Quaker to Catholic, you and I and everyone must practice this parameter of praying.

Confession in praying does not mean groveling in morbid introspection. Nor is confession a recitation of trivial peccadilloes. Furthermore, never think that confessing is a substitute for amending or changing your life. This parameter of praying, properly understood, is coming clean before God about yourself. Confession is dealing with the poison of guilt.

Charles de Foucauld led the harsh life of a French soldier in Algeria until he was cashiered from the army. He drifted around North Africa, living with a few different women from time to time, squandering his life. At the same time, he sensed that his inner restlessness came from his unsavory life. He returned to France, praying, "My God, if You exist, grant me to know You," but found no sense of God. One day, de Foucauld wandered into the confessional of a Paris church. He said to the priest, "I have not come to confess; I have no faith." The priest, a perceptive genius, replied, "It is not your faith, my friend, but your conscience that is at fault." Charles de Foucauld confessed. He was absolved. Cleansed by confessing, he later returned to Algeria as a Trappist monk. He served valiantly with the Little Brothers and the Little Sisters of the Poor in North Africa, becoming a legend for Christian compassion before being killed when the desert tribes revolted against the French.

Thanksgiving

The next parameter of praying is thanksgiving. Christians are realistic; they know how easy it is to forget that God is the Giver and Sustainer.

You will be tempted to attribute any success to your own efforts, or your good luck, thinking, "My power and the might of my hand have gotten me this . . ." (Deuteronomy 8:17). Like the rest of us, you will be shocked at your proclivity to congratulate yourself, Pharisee-style, when you pray.

You will also be surprised at how short your memory is when it comes to numbering God's blessings in the past. You will see something of yourself in the story of the ungrateful constituent of the late Senator and Vice-president Alben Barkley. As Barkley told the story, he was campaigning once in Breathitt County, Kentucky, when an old mountaineer told him to his face that he planned to vote for Barkley's opponent in the coming election. Barkley was disappointed.

"Why, Teecee," the senator said, "the first thing I did once I got to be senator was to make your Ma postmistress at Hardshell. I got your Uncle Jeb a job as deputy marshal in Lexington, and he can't even read. Last year I saw you got your crop loan, and when your Cousin Lily got in a family way a couple months ago, I sent her the government baby book."

"That's all true," said Teecee, "and I don't want you to think I've forgotten. But, Senator, what have you done for me lately?"

You and I suffer from the Teecee syndrome. We wonder what God has done for us lately—unless we can pray giving thanks.

"Pray constantly, give thanks in all circumstances; for this is the will of God in Christ Jesus for you," the Apostle Paul advised (1 Thessalonians 5:17,18). Give thanks for *everything*, for God's mercy through Jesus Christ, for the promise which a newborn baby brings and for the taste of a slice of fresh, homemade bread. Take an inventory of the causes for thanksgiving in your life each night before bed, and use that list in your praying.

Corrie ten Boom, the dauntless Dutch Christian imprisoned in a Nazi death camp, described how her sister, Betsie, insisted on giving thanks for everything, even during horrors of imprisonment. Corrie drew the line when it came to thanking God for the lice in their filthy, crowded barracks. Betsie, however, insisted that they pray thankfully even for lice. Corrie still had a problem including lice in their thanksgivings. It was not until later that they found that the lice prevented the brutal guards from entering Corrie's and Betsie's barracks and seizing their precious Bible and tiny hoard of forbidden supplies. Corrie ten Boom reluctantly decided that God's command, "Give thanks in all circumstances," even includes lice-filled concentration camp shacks!

Name your blessings—even the *lousy* kind—and pray with thanksgiving!

Supplication

When a former member of the British Parliament died, a written prayer was discovered among his papers. Apparently he took his praying seriously. The prayer, however, betrayed his greedy spirit. After buying a large piece of property at a cheap price because it was flooded, and after having the area drained at taxpayers' expense, this man prayed, "O Lord, Thou knowest I have an estate in the county of London and likewise that I have lately purchased an estate in the county of Essex. I beseech Thee to preserve the counties of Essex and Middlesex from fire and earthquake and, as I have a mortgage in Hertford, I beg Thee to have an eye of compassion on that county also. As for the rest of the counties, Thou mayest deal with them as Thou pleasest."

Perhaps not surprisingly, the person who prayed this prayer of supplication died broke. Actually, he was already spiritually and morally bankrupt when he petitioned the Lord so selfishly.

Prayers of supplication are not attempts to wheedle things from God for ourselves. Instead, they are to give God an opportunity to do what He wants with us!

Sören Kierkegaard, the Danish thinker, said it well, "The immediate person thinks and imagines that when he prays, the important thing, the thing he must concentrate upon, is that God should hear what he is praying for. And yet in the true, eternal sense, it is just the reverse: the true relation in prayer is not when God hears what is prayed for, but when the person praying continues to pray until he is the one who hears, who hears what God wills" (Sören Kierkegaard, *Journals of Soren Kierkegaard*).

Prayers of supplication are not begging prayers but cooperating prayers with God. You are not trying to change God's mind (as if that would be possible) or persuading Him to do what He does not intend to do. You are praying to change yourself, not God. "God does not ask us to tell Him our needs that He may learn about them, but in order that we may be capable of receiving what He is preparing to give," wrote St. Augustine in *Letters,* CXXX (To Flora), 17.

Some bystanders watched a one-legged veteran painfully drag himself up the steps to a chapel. As the cripple clumsily worked himself toward the door, one onlooker cynically commented, "What does he expect— that God will grow him a new leg?"

Overhearing the remark, the man without a leg turned and replied, "He always gives me enough to get along with the one I have."

Your prayers will also take the form of petitioning God from time to time. You will discover that God will sometimes say no to your requests. It may help you to remember that He also turned down the earnest prayers of supplication of people such as Moses, who prayed to live to enter the Promised Land, and Paul, who prayed that his thorn in the form of a painful, debilitating illness would be removed, and Jesus, who prayed fervently in Gethsemane that He would not have to drain the cup of suffering. You will also learn that God always gives you enough to get along on!

Adoniram Judson, the pioneering Baptist missionary to Burma, originally prayed to be able to go to India. Instead, he was sent to Burma. His wife became seriously ill, and Judson prayed earnestly for her life to be spared. Instead, the heartbroken missionary had to dig her grave himself. He also lost two children. He was arrested on trumped-up charges by suspicious, hostile authorities, and was forced to lie in a steaming, filthy oriental jail. In his misery, Judson prayed for release. Instead, he languished for months, forgotten, ill, and starving. Years later, at the close of his illustrious career, the great messenger quietly stated, "I have never prayed sincerely and earnestly for anything but it came; at some time—no matter how distant a day— somehow—in some shape—probably the last I should have devised—it came."

You, too, will discover the same when you learn the parameter of the prayer for supplication.

Intercession

Someone called my attention to a bathing beauty contest which was opened with prayer by a local preacher. I acknowledged that I would find myself somewhat uncertain how to pray for the contestants, and would personally prefer not to offer a public prayer on such an occasion. The other person, apparently disappointed, said, "Oh, well, it can't do any harm, I suppose."

"Can't do any harm." This is the notion of praying which many of us have. Tame and innocuous, we look upon it as a gesture, like flowers on Mother's Day. Praying, however, is actually as innocuous as mixing sulfur, potassium nitrate, and charcoal. Real praying has the explosive effect of gunpowder in our lives. Prayer blasts your selfishness so that you see others.

This is the significance of the prayer of intercession. You focus not on yourself but on others. And you are delivered from the crippling obsession with self.

An ancient legend in the Talmud tells of a person who said, "While I walked one day in the mountains, I saw at a distance what I took to be a beast. As I drew nearer, I saw it was a man. As I came nearer still, I discovered it was my brother." As you learn the meaning of intercessory prayer, your vision clears so that you see others not as beasts or even as people, but as sisters and brothers.

Brigitte Bardot, the pouty-faced French actress, announced recently, "I find my equilibrium in nature, in the company of animals. I hate humanity—I am allergic to it." Pathetically, she never has understood how God interceded for her on the Cross, and consequently cannot bring herself to choose to intercede for others. The aging sex kitten unhappily shuns all personal relationships and tries to live in seclusion.

The person who cannot or will not pray for others will end by hating not only others but God and self as well. Intercessory praying is divine preventative medicine to offset the constantly present tendency to turn in on yourself.

Don't ever underestimate the effect of your prayers for others. You may think you want scientific proof that your praying helps, or you may demand empirical evidence that intercessory prayer works. First of all, you should already realize that so-called experts with their logical, rational explanations have been wrong too many times. In 1836, for example, a learned man, Dr. Lardner, published a book in which he proved conclusively that a steamboat could never cross the ocean; the book came to America that same year on the first steamboat that crossed the Atlantic. In 1939, television was receiving its final touches from engineers, and NBC beamed an experimental telecast from the World's Fair in Flushing to Manhattan a few miles away. Professor Charles L. Dawes, a Harvard professor and as knowledgeable an expert as anyone, sniffed that television would never achieve popularity because it "must take place in a semidarkened room and demands continuous attention." Don't let the experts con you. Particularly, don't allow the so-called scientific outlook to put limits on your prayers for others. No one except God has final or complete knowledge. When it comes to praying for others, don't paralyze your prayers by insisting on absolute understanding of what your praying is doing. The primary thing is *pray!*

A good test for how sincere your prayers for others are is: How willing are you to do something for the ones for whom you are praying? If you are praying for someone who is in the hospital, for instance, are you prepared to help look after her children? If you are praying for the leaders in government, are you willing to acquaint yourself with the facts of issues and assume your civic responsibilities?

Intercede for others—on your knees and with your

hands! Love comes in many shapes, and intercessory prayer is one of the biggest helpings of love you can possibly share with your brother and sister.

Dedication

Eventually, your praying must assume the form of personal commitment to Jesus Christ. The parameters of dedication mean that you agree that as Lord, Christ is sole owner and controller of all that you are and have. Your prayers ultimately conclude with the recognition that a serious choice must be made in your life, and that your life is trivialized until you choose to dedicate yourself to Him as Lord.

The artist William Holman Hunt conducted painting classes for aspiring young artists in a picturesque location by a lake shore. One evening, Hunt saw that one of his pupils was spending all of his time making a detailed sketch of an old barn and was ignoring the brilliant sunset which he was supposed to be painting. Hunt stood beside his student and remarked, "Son, it won't be light for long. You've got to choose between painting the shingles on the barn and the sunset in God's sky. There's time for only one or the other. What is your choice?"

Shingles or sunsets? Isn't this the way it is in life? There is time for only one or the other.

You must consciously and willfully dedicate your energies, your time, your possessions, your abilities—your *all*—to this Lord. Otherwise, all these will be claimed by default by the enemy.

"The one concern of the devil," noted Samuel Chadwick, "is to keep Christians from praying. He fears nothing from prayerless studies, prayerless work, prayerless religion. He laughs at our toil, mocks at our wisdom, but trembles when we pray."

6 - The Problems of Praying

I have a problem in my praying. My mind wanders and I can't concentrate on prayer. What do I do when I sometimes don't feel like praying? How can I pray when I have doubts? It's so hard to find the "right words."

You will have problems in praying. At least you will if you are (a) human, and (b) honest. What do you do about your prayer problems?

First, identify what the problem is. Be specific. Is it that you are easily distracted? Is it that you don't feel close to God? Write down on the left margin of a piece of paper in a column called, Prayer Problem, what you think your prayer problem is.

Next, in a column just to the right of where you have listed your problem in praying, list the possible causes of your problem. To do this as quickly and realistically as possible, list the possible causes for your prayer problem under any of these categories.

Possible Causes of My Prayer Problem
External (outside myself)
Surroundings
Events
Persons
Other

Internal (inside myself)
Physical
Intellectual
Emotional
Spiritual-Moral

Do not pretend that you will always understand all the causes for your prayer problems, or to be able to pinpoint every cause. Also, allow for many errors because of your faulty judgment and self-deception. Don't let these human limitations stop you, however; try to dissect your prayer problem. As best you can, identify the cause for your problem by using the schema shown above.

Next, move to seek possible cures. Using the list of possible outside and inside causes for your prayer problem, sift out ways of remedying the situation. List feasible solutions in a new column, located next to the column labeled Possible Causes. Make sure that your new column, called Possible Cures, contains only those which are clearly not hurtful to others or selfish.

Finally, begin a fourth column. Head it, Commitments. This list will include the definite promises you are making to the Lord and to yourself about solving the problems in your praying. These promises will be distilled from your list of Possible Cures.

Your page will look similar to this:

PRAYER PROBLEM
Define specific problem.

POSSIBLE CAUSES
External

Surroundings   State specifically what, if this applies.

Events   List precisely, if this is the case.

Persons   State exactly who, if you think someone is the cause of your problem.

Other

Internal

Physical   List any, if applicable.

Intellectual   Put down your doubts or questions, if these are causing you difficulty in praying.

Emotional   Write these down.

Spiritual-Moral   Come clean; write down *any* person you are not right with, or any practice you have which does not square with what you know God expects of you.

POSSIBLE CURES
List whatever you think might feasibly be done to remove the causes of your prayer problems, making

sure that your possible cures will not harm others or
yourself.

COMMITMENTS

State the four or five steps you are determined to
take from the list of possible cures. Then keep these
commitments!

Let's now look at some of the most common problems in praying, and reflect on the causes and cures.

Distractions

You have probably already remarked to yourself that
it is hard to concentrate on praying. You find yourself
easily distracted. You may be comforted somewhat by
knowing that even saintly John Donne once confessed,
"I neglect God and his angels for the noise of a fly, for
the rattling of a coach, for the whining of a door."

Some of your concentration problems in praying
such as fatigue or noise can readily be pigeonholed
under the heading, External Causes. If you are distracted from prayer primarily by the telephone and the
kids, take steps accordingly. One woman simply sets
her alarm and gets up a half hour before the family each
morning in order to have a few moments of uninter-
rupted Bible reading, contemplation, and praying.

What about the distractions which are externally
caused, but you cannot control, such as clanging by the

garbage collector or crying by a baby? Use these as
props for praying and meditating. For example, when
distracted by the garbage man, remember that we
waste so much food that we have the biggest, most
filled garbage cans in the world, and turn your prayers
toward the half of our world's people who would ea-
gerly pick through those garbage cans in order to find
the food they do not have. That crying baby may serve
to remind you of the millions of babies, crying in Asia
and Africa because of disease and malnutrition, who
will not be comforted or stilled—ever.

You may also find yourself having difficulty concen-
trating on praying because of internal causes. You may
be on the outs with someone, or you may have a persis-
tent habit which you secretly know is wrong. These fall
in the category of moral or spiritual causes. You will find
that they are like a nagging pebble in your shoe. You
may try to ignore it and pretend that it isn't there. You
may tell yourself that it's insignificant. But eventually,
you'll find yourself limping, hurting, and slowed. You
must remove the distracting moral stones crippling
your prayer life before you can concentrate.

One final word of advice on distractions in praying.
Do not wait until you are free of distractions before you
begin praying. Frankly, you never will be completely
away from both external and internal causes which dis-
tract. Although they interrupt your concentration on
praying, you do not need to let them stop you from
praying. As Martin Luther once said of temptation, you

may also say of distractions, "You cannot keep the birds from flying overhead but you can keep them from nesting in your hair!"

Dry Spells

You will also go through times when you will not feel very religious or when God will not seem very real or close. Your mood will not always be prayerful. You will be tempted to skip praying.

You with all the saints will also go through the "dark night of the soul" from time to time. When you experience these times when praying comes slow and hard, "Wait on the Lord: be of good courage, and he shall strengthen thine heart" (Psalms 27:14 KJV). Hang on! Refreshment is promised! Like the thirsty person who struggles across the desert and gives up just short of the oasis, you may quit too soon. Keep going; keep praying!

How often in history has victory been snatched up by the jaws of defeat when people stopped just short of success. In World War I, the British fleet failed to press through the strait of the Dardanelles and settled down for a long stalemate and eventual withdrawal. After the war, naval leaders discovered how a little more perseverance and determination would have easily brought them victory—and perhaps a quicker end to the war. "I never realized how near we were," they regretfully kept telling one another afterward.

You will never realize how near you are to the One who keeps His word with those who persevere in prayer, unless you keep on praying. "They that wait upon the Lord shall renew their strength" (Isaiah 40:31 KJV) you will discover.

The times when you may not feel like praying are the exact times when you most need to pray. Do not wait until you psych yourself into a religious mood. Pray! Remember Francis de Sales' words about spiritual dry spells: "The prayer that is most acceptable to God is that which we make by force and constraint, the prayer to which we consign ourself not for any relish we find in it, nor by inclination, but purely to please God; to which our will carries us against our inclinations, violently forcing its way through the midst of the dryness . . . which opposes it."

Doubts and Questions

You will also find you will have doubts and questions as you try to pray. Even Luther, unable to understand why he should have such severe pain in the midst of his illness in 1537, issued an ultimatum to the Lord: "If this pain lasts longer, I shall go mad and fail to recognize Thy goodness." You will wonder why you have pain. You will be perplexed at the setbacks and frustrations in life. Like the cynical king of Samaria, you may grumble, "This trouble is from the Lord! Why should I wait for the Lord any longer?" (2 Kings 6:33). The external events will cause you some internal problems in praying.

Some of your intellectual problems with praying turn

out to be the result of your immature thinking about God and prayer. For instance, part of the antireligious propaganda in the Soviet Union includes providing two side by side plots, and having the school children plant flowers and vegetables in each plot. The youngsters are instructed to pray over the one, asking God to make the plants grow. Nothing is done with this plot. On the other plot, there are no prayers said at all. However, the children are made to fertilize, weed, cultivate, and water the plants on this plot. The atheistic leaders smugly *prove* that prayer is useless and God is nonexistent by pointing to the difference between the two gardens. Some of your difficulties in praying may come from such silly notions of praying and God.

A man who had had a serious drinking problem joined Alcoholics Anonymous. After being sober for two weeks, he prayed demanding that God give him a good job. He did not get a good job. Puzzled and annoyed, he paraded his misgivings about prayer. It was not until a year later that he learned to handle his impatience and resentment in constructive ways. Humbly, the man confessed later, "I wasn't ready for a good job. I had lots to learn. God wasn't slow. He knew exactly what He was doing."

In your doubting and questioning, remember that God came to us not as a psycho but as a Saviour. He was not so devoted to self that He set pain on others. Rather, He was so devoted to others that He accepted others' pain on Himself.

Alfred North Whitehead, the English philosopher,

experienced the devastating loss of his eighteen-year-old son, Eric, in the WWI trenches in March, 1918. Whitehead's world was shattered. Even his great intellect could not provide answers to the mysteries of death. Later, however, he described his pilgrimage of faith. "It runs through three stages, if it evolves to its final satisfaction," Whitehead wrote; "it is the transition from God the void to God the enemy, and from God the enemy to God the companion."

Your intellectual problems *may* be a smoke screen. Your doubts *may* be dodges. Your questions *may* be excuses for refusing to trust. Ultimately, you must make the transition from God the void to God the companion. And with the Companion, you have enough! Meanwhile, however, your real problem in praying may well be that you do not want God messing around in your life. Max Scheler, the German thinker, put it well: "Even if it could be proved by mathematics that God exists, I do not want Him to exist because He would set limits to my greatness." Your problems in prayer may well be that you do not want the Lord setting limits to your greatness.

The Problem Behind Your Problems

The root problem in praying for you and me and every person is alienation. You are alienated from God. You are alienated from others. And you are alienated from yourself.

You are alienated from the Parent-God because you

cannot bear to face Him with your sordid little secrets. In your most lucid moments, you sense that you are known, that He knows all about you. You have the nagging sense that He has firsthand awareness of your greedy schemes, your cheap excuses, your white lies, your oily rationalizations, your sneaky self-righteousness, your impure motives, and your disguised anger. You cannot stand God because you cannot stand being found out for what you are. This is why people like you and me crucified Jesus; they couldn't stand His telling the truth about themselves so they killed Him.

Do you remember how airline passengers in the early days of baggage inspections before the advent of electronic screening devices were forced to submit their luggage to minute scrutiny? Many blushed or bridled at emptying the contents of purses, suitcases, and briefcases on the counter for everyone to see. You have the same reluctance and resentment toward God probing your dark corners and intruding on your privacy. You don't like Him interfering in your affairs in any way.

You are already found out, however. You can only pray, "O Lord, thou hast searched me, and known me!" (Psalms 139:1 KJV).

Yet, astonishingly, this Searcher and Knower accepts you in love! This is the Gospel.

You might have been telling yourself that prayer is irksome. You possibly have been glad for any excuse to avoid the encounter with the One. Secretly you might have welcomed interruptions in your praying so that you would not have to allow the Searcher and Knower to get too close. You might have jumped up with relief whenever prayer was over because you would not have to risk being discovered. You might have stated that prayer has so many problems when, actually, the real problem was that you did not want to be dethroned. In truth, you could not stand God. He threatened your sovereignty. Therefore, you pushed Him as far away as you could. You repudiated Him and His rule.

Repudiating the One who must be the very center of your being, you could not stand yourself or others. Here is where your prayer problem really began.

God, however, persists in overcoming every problem which prevents Him from having fellowship with you. He even returned Jesus from the grave! He insisted on personally handling the problem of your alienation and shame by sending the Risen Lord to you. No problem is too great for this God to handle, not even the huge problem of your guilt. God already has dealt with every problem which separates you from Him. If your heart condemns you and keeps you from praying, God is greater than your heart!

7-The Price of Praying

In an age of instant gratification, we all have joined the Now Generation. We insist on speedy, easy results. Most of us have slumped into being passive spectators at everything—including prayer. Even God, we assume, must render *Quick Service*, with little effort on our part.

You already realize the need for disciplined commitment in sports, music, a graduate degree, or an elite combat group. Look at the endless practice hours behind an Olympic medal. Consider a star performer's dedication to tedious weeks of rehearsals for a show. Note how your doctor must put in 150 hours of hard-nosed study each year to stay accredited. You must be prepared to invest the same kind of single-minded devotion to your praying.

Have you considered the cost of praying? Are you aware that meaningful prayer means paying a price? Or, in your prayer life, are you as casual and hasty as the tourist on a rush tour of Europe who screeched to a stop in front of Chartres Cathedral, jumped out, and called to his wife, "You take the inside, I'll do the outside.

Meet you here in five minutes." You will never understand or appreciate praying without a disciplined and
careful effort. After all, you are meant to be embarking
on a relationship, and relationships—especially genuine ones which are fragile and growing—demand commitment.

You must be prepared to undertake a *Protestant
monasticism.* You may understand this modern monasticism as a contemporary form of the traditional vows
of poverty, chastity, and obedience.

Self-denial

Your life as a modern monastic will run counter to
our hedonistic culture. Frankly, you will be out of ca-
dence with the pampered pleasure seekers who are our
pacesetters in styles and ideas. Your monasticism will
not make a cult of pain for pain's sake. You will not be
involved in the sick forms of asceticism which are
obsessively self-centered and destructive.

The neurotic, self-mortifying, early Christian her-
mits, with their unwholesome, negative preoccupation
with their sex drives, despised their creatureliness and
the world. Be careful that you do not show contempt
toward your body or the earth—which God has pronounced "Good" (Genesis 1:31). The model for your
monasticism is Jesus, who voluntarily gave for others.

Your monasticism is not another do-it-yourself salva-
tion kit. You should already realize that you can never

hope to impress God sufficiently to earn divine grace. None of your sweaty efforts at being religious will ever buy you a better standing with the Lord. Your so-called sacrifices can be subtle forms of ego massage. You are saved by grace. But you must also cooperate with grace!

A contemporary Christian monasticism calls for simplicity in life-style as an up-to-date form of the traditional vow of poverty. Remember that as Americans in today's world village, you are only 6 percent of the globe's population, but consume 40 percent of its resources. You must studiously seek to share. In the name of the One who "for your sake he became poor" (*see* 2 Corinthians 8:9), you must adopt a philosophy contrary to the acquisitive-consumer mentality of our world.

As a modern monastic, you do not renounce the marriage relationship; rather, you live within it. True chastity does not mean ignoring your sexuality or dismissing your biological drives as evil or labeling the sex act as dirty or funny. The self-denial behind meaningful praying calls for a caring commitment to your partner in marriage for as long as he or she is alive.

Stillness

We live in such a noise polluted environment that sixteen million Americans suffer from boilermakers' disease—a condition in which there is partial hearing loss accompanied by weight loss, fatigue, and even impaired sexuality. Thirty-five million Americans live in areas where the twenty-four-hour noise level averages sixty-five decibels, which is classified as annoying. Ninety percent of the United States population is subjected to sporadic intrusive sounds exceeding seventy-five decibels. And the sound is rising at an estimated rate of 10 percent each year. Even the wilderness winter silences are now defiled by snowmobiles.

The construction of an inner life demands periods of quiet. If your personal authenticity comes from God, you must have the stillness to contemplate the mystery of His mercy to you, which in turn gives you an understanding of the mystery of your being.

In the British Navy, when a disaster occurs, the boatswain pipes what is called *the still.* This signal requires every seaman and officer to stand stock-still in a moment of enforced calm. *The still* prevents panic and alerts each man to wait for further instructions.

You must have your own time for *the still* in which you stand by and listen for orders. Such quiet is a prerequisite for you to grow in prayer. Your style of monasticism means a self-discipline in which you deliberately shut out the noises and voices and sounds that constantly assault you.

You may, for example, deliberately refuse to turn on the radio or television during a certain point of your daily routine, thereby escaping the sound bath which threatens to drown your awareness of the One who is the Word. One man, who commutes to and from work, finds his car to be one of the few places where he can partially isolate himself from the sounds of telephones, Muzak, and newscasts, and cherishes the comparative quiet as a period to reflect and pray. Or, like many, you may accept the monastic duty of early rising in order to find an oasis of silence in the noisy day. Abigail Adams, wife of President John Adams, regularly got up at 5:00 A.M. in order to get a period of stillness in which to pray, read, and reflect, even though she had the constant burdens of a family household and a farm to manage. You also will have to elect to discipline yourself to cut out zones of silence in your schedule.

In the days of the desert fathers, a wise elder used to ask a newly arrived novice to bring a bowl of water from a desert pool. Placing the bowl of murky liquid on the ground, the two would sit and watch the sediment settle and the water finally become clear. Turning to the novice, the older monk would say, "Your own life has been like that turbid water. But if you enter the silence with God, your heart will become clean like this water. And you will be able to reflect God who can only be seen and known by the pure in heart."

Solitude

You must also devise stratagems for privacy. Unless you have moments to be alone with the Alone, you will probably never grow in your relationship. You must have some solitude and interiority.

Unfortunately, such aloneness runs contrary to the

current fad for togetherness. Even offices and schools are now designed without partitions. Loners are suspect. Perceptive souls, however, recognize how indispensable privacy is. The New Zealand Antarctic party on McMurdo Sound, realizing the necessity to shut out the signs and sounds of others, especially when forced to live in close proximity for long periods of time, designed its polar huts so that without loss of space each man had a tiny private cubicle into which he could go and bolt the door.

Many old Pennsylvania Dutch farmhouses were built with a prayer closet, a small cubbyhole adjacent to an upstairs room, designed as a place for undisturbed contemplation. Although your prayer place need not be of brick, wood, or plaster, you must be able to closet yourself. Jesus advised, "But when you pray, go into your room and shut the door and pray to your Father who is in secret; and your Father who sees in secret will reward you" (Matthew 6:6).

As a modern monastic, you will have to show an obedience to Jesus by seeking solitude regularly. You will find that this may require exceptional ingenuity; however, you can succeed. You may wish to follow the lead of J. Arthur Rank, the British film producer, who refused to ride the elevator in his studio in order to walk up to his office. When asked why he chose to plod by himself up the long flights of steps, Rank smiled and replied that they were what he called his *prayer stairs*. Or, you may take a tip from several commuters who must ride a bus or train to their jobs, and turn this empty block of time often filled with snoozing, chatting, or headline-scanning into a welcome cocoon of seclusion. Robert E. Speer, a longtime church executive under the heavy pressure of schedule and decisions, wrote the devotional classic, *Five Minutes A Day,* over a period of several years during the solitude seized while on his daily commuting run to and from New York. Or, if you sometimes have trouble sleeping, instead of fretfully gulping pills and tossing restlessly, regard this as a God-given bonus period of isolation. Use those minutes as an occasion for being in secret with the Father.

System

A system is an interconnected, interdependent series of sub-parts that function together. You must regard prayer as part of the system of the life of faith. This is what Paul has in mind when he counsels his converts, "Pray without ceasing" (1 Thessalonians 5:17 KJV).

"Pray without ceasing" does not mean that you are to be perpetually on your knees. Rather, you are to consider your life of praying exactly the way a crack professional tennis player or a leading opera star regards his or her career. Everything that the athlete or vocalist does is tied in with playing or singing. There are times of intense exercise, on the practice court or at the keyboard in the practice room. Even when not holding a racquet or trilling an aria, the star watches his or her diet and sleep. Posture, breathing, and gait are considered. The pro is influenced in every part of everyday living, directly or indirectly, by a zeal and purpose, and constantly keeps career in mind. On the field or off, on stage or off, everything in life is part of the system of tennis or the system of opera. The dedicated performer plays without ceasing or sings without ceasing, knowing that success comes from having all the interconnected, interdependent series of sub-parts functioning together.

This is the way your life of prayer must be regarded, as a system. Prayer is not a minor compartment filed under the heading of *religion*. As a Protestant monastic, become systematic in your praying.

Structure

You will not always feel like praying. Neither does the tennis champ nor the opera star always feel like playing or singing. The flame of commitment flares and sputters, and flares again. Just because you do not feel prayerful does not mean that you quit praying. In fact, the feeling may be interpreted as a warning signal that you are actually in more need of God than you realize.

As a Protestant monastic, you must develop the prayer habit so that praying is structured into your living. "Place yourself in the presence of God" *("Mettez-vous en la présence de Dieu")* counsels Francis de Sales at the beginning of every one of his meditations. He means that you must firmly put yourself to praying, even when you may not have prayerful inclinations or when God may not seem very close.

William Law, who was another who arose at 5:00 A.M., would repeat, "When I awake, I am still with Thee." Note that he did not say, "When I awake I *feel* that I am still with Thee." Law wisely did not consult his feelings, because he knew that there were some mornings when he was groggy and cold. Instead, with the structure which true praying must assume, he firmly announced to the Lord and himself, "I *am* with Thee."

Sometimes, you will find that visible acts and concrete imagery will help you put structure in your praying. Your Jewish friends, with *tallith* (prayer shawl) and *yarmulke* (head covering), concretize devotion in ways meaningful to them. Your Roman Catholic neighbors, by saying the rosary and looking at the crucifix, instill structure into their religious lives. You may either appropriate ceremonies and symbols of the Christian faith for your own use, or improvise some for yourself. For example, holding hands as a family around the table while repeating a memorized grace before eating (such as "Come Lord Jesus, Be Thou our Guest, Our morning Joy, our evening Rest. And with Thy daily bread impart Thy Love and Peace to every heart") symbolizes and ceremonializes the Living Lord in your midst in a way both children and parents may appreciate. Such is the stuff of structure in praying!

Schedule

You are already aware that time, like your money and energy, is limited. You must budget your hours even more carefully than your income. This means that you will have to arrange unbroken blocks of minutes for prayer and contemplation in your schedule. You simply cannot evade this obvious fact, and will discover that every person who came to have a meaningful prayer life had to discipline himself or herself to a schedule.

For example, John Wesley, undoubtedly one of the busiest and most productive Christians ever, learned early that praying presumes a method (and, with his friends, won the nickname *Methodists* as a result.) Wesley kept diaries, scores of which are preserved today. On the first page of each, Methodist John Wesley inscribed this vow: "I resolve, *Deo juvante*, (1) to devote an hour morning and evening to private prayer, no pretense, no excuse whatsoever; and (2) to converse κατὰ θεόν (face to face with God), no lightness, no εὐτραπελία (facetiousness)." Wesley accurately calculated the price he had to pay for praying.

Your schedule, of course, is not the same as Wesley's or anyone else's. Only you can plan periods for prayer. But, you must plan! Perhaps you are a morning person —one whose metabolism is functioning, eyes are bright, and step is bouncy as soon as you get up in the morning—but even if you are not, you may find the only time you can schedule praying is early in the day.

In turn, this may mean disciplining yourself to retire earlier the night before. Your hair shirt may be to miss the eleven o'clock news and the late show.

Experts in time management teach that you must have ninety-minute chunks of time for creative thinking. Executives are trained to block out ninety-minute periods regularly. During these time segments, almost no interruptions are permitted. ("Nobody is to bother me on the telephone during that time except my wife and the president of the United States," reports one business leader, adding with a smile, "and my wife knows not to call then and I'm not expecting any calls from the White House.")

You will have to budget at least one ninety-minute block each week. Perhaps an evening is the best time when you must determine to turn aside from the spirit-anesthetizing cycle of televised detective mysteries and situation comedies, and to avoid resolutely the tentacle embrace of committees, clubs, bowling league and, yes, even church meetings for that one night. During that ninety-minute time frame, you may begin to understand the form of prayer known as contemplation.

Praying as contemplation is not woolgathering. Contemplation means listening, reflecting, jotting down your thoughts about God and your life in a journal, and engaging in serious Bible reading.

Time for contemplation permits the Spirit to be at work, gently, and unobtrusively. A few years ago, marine salvage men struggled to raise a small vessel which had sunk in a deep part of a harbor. They tried hoisting the sunken ship with cables and winches and unsuccessfully tried pumping air into its chambers, but nothing worked until a young engineer came up with a startlingly simple solution. At low tide, lines were firmly attached to the wreck from a number of barges moored above. As the tide came in, the barges floating on the surface raised the hulk below, and were pushed easily to a safer and more shallow location. Unseen forces were allowed to take over. Basically, contemplation allows the tides of the Presence to flow into your life and to raise your problems from the unmanageable depths. Slowly, quietly, almost unnoticed, His powerful nearness comes—when you discipline your life.

Perhaps you secretly dream of getting away from it all somehow, someplace, someday, and taking time to perch alone on a silent peak high above the disruptive clatter of civilization. Forget it! Even the Matterhorn, once the symbol for solitude, now has so many tourists scaling the steep slopes that the Zermatt guides have had to declare strict time limits for silent contemplation at the top. Climbers are permitted only forty-five minutes on the summit before they must move off to make room for the next group. Are parking meters next? You must create your own private mountain tops in your day by day, week by week routine. Your prayer life is your only Matterhorn to which you may retreat. You must prepare to pay the stiff price for praying. It costs.

You will have to invest heavily by bartering your time, your energies, your self-interest. However, "Love so amazing, so divine," as the old hymn says it, "demands your life, your soul, your all!"

8-The Pilgrimage of Praying

Recently, a close friend of mine died. Dusty and I had shared common ties to Scotland since both of us had studied in Edinburgh, and we had shared a common interest in books since both of us had served in academic institutions. A few weeks after Dusty's death, his widow suddenly took ill and also died. The only survivors were a couple of distant cousins in Canada. To settle the estate as quickly as possible, it was decided to auction everything. Some of us who were his friends went to Dusty's house on the morning of the sale. Furniture, books, diplomas, clothing, tools, dishes, pictures, personal mementos from years of travels and teaching, and even the knickknacks from Dusty's desk were strewn everywhere in the yard for people to pick over and examine before bidding.

What brought tears to the eyes of those of us who knew Dusty best, however, was seeing his prized academic gown, the brilliant scarlet Edinburgh robe with its doctoral chevrons on the sleeves, cast carelessly on a chest from the basement beside a box of old medicine bottles. That robe, which represented years of sacrifice

for research, and symbolized decades of devoted service while teaching, now lay contemptuously thrown
aside like the discarded basement junk and used pre-
scription bottles. Dusty's robe, like his beloved books
and keepsakes, his university position, his desk and furniture, car and house, were all passed on to someone
else.

You also, will have to leave behind your dear ones,
your job, and your prized possessions. Although it is an
unsettling experience, you should put yourself through
the discipline of writing your own obituary. Yes, write
your own obituary just as you think it will appear someday in the newspaper. Set down the date and the age
you think you will be when you die. Write the place, the
cause of your death, and your survivors. Also state what
you think you will be chiefly remembered for, as a
newspaper reporter would list it. Then read your obituary.

Alfred Nobel, the inventor of dynamite, was shaken
to read of his own death one morning in 1888. What
had happened was that Alfred's brother had died, but
a careless reporter had assumed that it was the famous
explosives tycoon. Alfred Nobel was startled to see what
the world really thought of him. His obituary referred
to him as the "merchant of death" and the "dynamite
king." The public would remember him only for amass-
ing a huge fortune based on the destructive use of his
famous invention, Nobel discovered. He immediately
summoned his attorneys and made arrangements to

change the way he used his enormous wealth. Because Nobel read his own obituary that day, he is remembered today as the person who devoted his life and billions to the cause of international peace, symbolized in the world famous prizes that bear his name, the Nobel Prize.

The point of obituary reading is not to be morbid, but in the face of the fragility and brevity of life, to set your priorities. You must contemplate the fact that some day, you will be stripped of everything—your family, your friends, your titles, your positions, your responsibilities, your surroundings, and even your body. Until you go through the needle's eye of the meaning of death, you cannot deal with life.

Life is bound by horizons. The final horizon is death. Your possibilities ultimately are limited by that eventual horizon. Until you recognize what the thinker Martin Heidegger called "the iron ring round existence" you are not able to begin your pilgrimage of life.

"Men are in danger of forgetting that they who rightly practice philosophy study nothing else than dying and death," wrote Plato (*Phaedo*, 64). You must examine the possibilities still open to you, knowing that all human and earthly things come to an end before they are perfected or completed.

Until you can be alone with *nothing*, until you recognize how terribly vulnerable you are, until the real *you* is laid bare, life will not become a pilgrimage. Only as you are aware of your own impending death will your life be shown for what it is. Only when you have contemplated existence apart from everything except the one God, will life be clarified. You must be shaken out of your indifference and your indolence.

When you consider the needle's eye experience, you will react in one of three ways. You will react to the eventuality of your own death either (1) by deceit, (2) by despair, or (3) by devotion. If you are deceiving yourself, others, or God, you are playacting ("hypocrite," Jesus says!) and your prayer life will be a sham and a shambles. If you react to death with despair, you cannot stand God. You cannot stand others. And you cannot stand yourself. Despair destroys. Ultimately, the destructive forms of despair are death: genocide—killing others; deicide—murdering God (and this is the partial meaning of the Crucifixion); and suicide—destroying self.

The other possibility is devotion to the Giver, Sustainer, and Renewer of life. Apart from a pilgrimage of devotion to that Resurrected and Resurrecting Lord, you will end by default in deceit or despair. Your life, therefore, is more than an aimless counting off the years until the undertaker comes. Your life beginning *now* is meant to be a pilgrimage of praying!

Companions on Your Pilgrimage

To continue growing in your pilgrimage of praying, you must have companions. Your fellow pilgrims, should include some who are alive and physically near you and also some who will become cherished associates through their writings.

Prayer groups sometimes become elitist and cliquish. Nonetheless, you will find your pilgrimage made less lonely by convenanting with a half dozen or more others to meet weekly to study Scripture, to share concerns, and to pray for each other. From personal experience, you will learn that your fellow pilgrims will aid you more in your praying than reading shelves of books on prayer.

For one thing, your co-pilgrims in your prayer caravan will help keep you honest in praying! Jane Addams, the pioneer Christian social worker in Chicago's Hull House, used to take some of her Hull House women with her whenever she had to meet with aldermen, the Chicago city council, or other officials to talk about conditions on Halsted Street because, she maintained, these women served to keep her from being deflected from the needs of the neighborhood. Just as Jane Addams' Halsted Street friends helped remind her of the right issues, your prayer associates will help you avoid the phony stuff which can sidetrack you.

Your praying companions will also help keep you from being inverted in your prayer life. In fact, a real test of any prayer group is whether or not the members are others directed or ourselves directed. Here is where you may enroll in the school of intercessory prayer. Your praying in a group may take on the dimension of interceding for others instead of yourself.

Intercessory prayer, you will discover, means loving your neighbor on your knees. Praying for others is cooperating with God's saving, strengthening power.

You really never know the extent to which you are already affecting those around you. In India recently, a villager dropped the carcass of a dead animal down a neighbor's well to retaliate for a hurt. To his surprise and pain, he made himself, his own family, and the whole village deathly sick. The man did not know of the underground chambers which flowed from one well to another. Polluting his neighbor's water supply, he also poisoned himself. Your concern or your lack of concern for others has a powerful effect on your neighbors and on yourself. You already have an intimate association and an interdependent relationship with everyone else in the world village. Praying for others helps clear some of the springs of our common life dangerously clogged with the toxic powers of hate, greed, violence, prejudice, cynicism, fear, and guilt.

Companions in your pilgrimage are necessary, but they may never take the place of your commitment to the others in the household of Christ's people, especially your local congregation. You will have to face frankly the temptation to regard your prayer group as a cozy crew of super-Christians and as a substitute for the Church. The *we-versus-they* syndrome sneaks in subtly. You will sometimes have to steel yourself to stay with the organized and institutionalized Christianity, especially when it declines into dreary churchianity.

You are undoubtedly expert at picking out the examples of spiritual blight and stunted growth in your local church. You recoil at the stupidity and the cussedness of some of those Christians. Probably you would like to turn your back on your fellow church members. Remember, however, that God has not written them off, even though you may! If they are good enough for God to send Christ to die for on the Cross, they are good enough for you! And your own personal cross may be staying with the Church. You may have to crucify your pride and your dignity on behalf of those gossipy, petty-minded hypocrites who sing off-key and never pray enough. Christ's call, among other things, means a call for you to remain covenanted with the others in His family, the Church. They need you. And, whether you realize it or not, you also need them!

Other Companions: Authors

Fellow pilgrims on your pilgrimage of praying must also include some whom you will meet only through reading. Topping the list of your reading, of course, is the Bible. You will discover in The Book that God is the chief Author-Actor in the script of life. Astonishingly, as you read, you discover that He writes you into the story. Through the Scripture's words, He who is the Word communicates to *you.* The episodes described in Scripture become *your* story. Abraham, Jacob, Moses,

Joshua, David, Elijah, Isaiah, Jeremiah, Peter, John, and Paul—all these and a host of others become contemporaries and helpers. Most of all, the Risen Lord, the Pilgrim who has already blazed the trail of the pilgrimage and walks it with you, presents Himself through Scripture and sacrament.

Your Bible is indispensable. As Dwight L. Moody, the American evangelist, once wrote in the flyleaf of a man's Bible: "This Book will keep you from your sins, or your sins will keep you from this Book."

You will also want to associate with other pilgrims through books. Sooner or later, you should meet such persons as St. Augustine (354–430 A.D.) who shared his thoughts in a journal known as *Confessions;* Bernard of Clairvaux (1091–1153) who wrote *On Consideration;* Thomas à Kempis (1380–1471) who transcribed the classic *The Imitation of Christ,* the all-time devotional best-seller; Francis de Sales (1567–1622) who penned the practical *Introduction to the Devout Life;* Brother Lawrence (1666–1728) the kitchen worker-monk who shared his secret in *The Practice of the Presence of God;* William Law (1686–1761); Soren Kierkegaard (1813–1855), and others.

As a pilgrim, you will sense sometimes loneliness and uneasiness. As you associate with the authors of some of the devotional classics, you will find friendship and encouragement. You will find yourself interacting with, listening to, and praying with pilgrims through the ages. Learning about their struggles, you also learn about your own. You find that they personalize truth about the relationship with the Other.

You and I, still in the kindergarten stage of prayer, are just beginning to put together the blocks to spell the simplest words of praying. More experienced pilgrims such as Thomas à Kempis teach not theological theories but the curriculum of life with Christ.

On your praying pilgrimage, you need nourishment. These classics feed you. Forget the devotional best-sellers, the current *in* literature of various prayer groups. Some of these are merely diluted broth from the richer meat and vegetables of Scripture and the great writers. Other devotional literature, like sugary breakfast cereal in expensive packaging, consists of sweet-tasting filler with little lasting nutriment and provides a bit of quick energy which is soon burned up but deprives you of needed growth food. The Augustines and Kierkegaards offer you new symbols and new insights for you to ingest for strength and maturation in praying.

Fellowship with God that Spills Over

How can you grow in your prayer life? In addition to finding companions for the pilgrimage, you must share with others. Your relationship with God must result in concern for others. You cannot hoard the love of God to yourself. It spills over. You are sent to heal the hurts of the world.

True prayer is not escaping from the world. Some

mistakenly think that prayer is a substitute for serving. If praying takes the place of serving, it becomes a cop-out. (On the other hand, if serving takes the place of praying, it becomes busywork!) Praying and serving go together. It is never a choice of one or the other, but always *both*.

If you try to pull a Jonah-like cop-out by refusing to get involved in the Nineveh around you, God firmly prods you. He insists that you take up your responsibilities for others. God never permits you the luxury of praying without getting involved. "Oh, but I don't want to get all mixed up in the dirty old world," you say. Look at how God deliberately got Himself mixed up with the dirty old world of dying slaves in the Egyptian brick yards in Moses' day, in the affairs of a peasant couple and some frightened shepherds in a stable in Bethlehem, among the hungry hordes on a Galilee hillside late one day, with feverish youngsters and anxious parents, and with crippled beggars and crowded streets! God took up residence in human form on this planet. God chose to be involved. He also insists that your prayers become incarnated in service. If you try to escape serving others in the world, He will refuse to grant you peace no matter how persistently or eloquently you beseech Him.

Your concern for others through prayer and service must be specific. You may find it mildly satisfying to pray for others in generalities. In fact, you may get a certain sense of pride out of vague foggy prayers for the sick and shut-ins. Be definite! "St. Francis did not love humanity but men," G. K. Chesterton, English novelist, remarked correctly. Love without focus degenerates into Don Juanism. Express your concerns by using names. And give legs and arms to your concern for others by doing!

During World War II, on one of those countless minor fronts which received little notice, ugly skirmishes occasionally took place in the mountainous border between France and Italy. In many of the Alpine valleys in that area, small, struggling congregations of Waldensian Christians still live. The Waldensian movement, which antedates the Reformation, produced the first *Protestants,* steel-willed Christians who insisted on taking their Lord at His word. One late autumn day during the War, French and Italian troops fought a short but fierce battle in one of the Waldensian villages. The French invaders ravaged the village, killing and wounding several villagers, and destroying precious houses, barns, and equipment. The Italian forces, after repelling the thrust, withdrew hurriedly, fearful of getting trapped in the severe snows in the mountains. The French also retreated, but left behind more than two hundred wounded.

Food was short. The Waldenses were desperately poor. Winter was approaching. There was no word from anyone about the forgotten enemy survivors. Powerful fires of vengeance burned in the hearts of most villagers. Some proposed shooting the invaders.

Others suggested abandoning them to the snows. The village leaders, however, remembered that they were Waldenses, and that meant saving, not destroying men's lives.

At grave personal risk the Waldensian mountain men undertook the exhausting task of piggybacking the wounded Frenchmen over a high Alpine pass, ferrying the enemy down steep paths until they came to the French border. While carrying the men who had fought against them and oppressed them, the Waldenses knew that they might slip and plunge to their deaths on the treacherous descent. They knew that they might be caught in an early blizzard and freeze to death on the icy heights. They also knew that they might be stopped by an Italian patrol and shot for collaborating with the enemy. The villagers knew, too, that they might be picked off on the ridges by enemy sharpshooters or machine-gunned as they approached the border.

The Waldenses, however, accepted the odds and made the grim journey with the two hundred enemy wounded. Depositing their human burdens in a deserted area, the village men contacted the French and withdrew safely. The exhausted Waldenses then recrossed the treacherous pass and descended into the mountain fastness of their homes. As they plodded wearily into their village, the villagers started to cheer. The old pastor silenced the cheering. What these men had done, he reminded everybody, was not noble or courageous. They were simply being Christians. It was, he told them, the only way that they had the right to pray, Our Father.

Praying must spill over in active service of others. If you want to grow in prayer, you will also carry the burdens of your sisters and brothers. As you serve others as well as pray, you discover the Spirit bestows little notes of grace at surprising intervals. Those grace notes in the score cheer you when you most need encouragement. You discover that it is in dying for others you are born to eternal life!

Burning the Boats

When the Spanish explorer Hernando Cortez landed in Mexico in 1519 with a mutinous crew, he burned his own ships in the Santiago harbor so that he would not be tempted to retreat to Spain in case of failure or defeat. He had no choice but to advance.

You must continue your pilgrimage of praying with the same kind of boat-burning resolve. You will often be tempted to quit. You will know failure and defeat. You will face almost constant struggle with self-interest.

"Believe me," wrote one of the earliest pilgrims, "I think there is nothing which requires more effort than to pray to God . . . Prayer demands combat to the last breath" *(Apophthegms of the Fathers.)*

Your combat will be most often with the divided heart, the half-loyalty, the qualified allegiance, the backward glance, the reluctant affirmation, the secret temptation, the splintered intention, the gnawing doubt, and the lurking despair in your life. True prayer, however, "is a struggle with God in which one triumphs through the triumph of God" (Kierkegaard, *Journals,* I).

You triumph through the triumph of God! As you continually commit yourself to Him in renewing your pilgrimage in praying, you find that He is at both ends of your praying. God is the Beginning and the End, the Initiator and the Completer. The Triumphant One, who is the Alpha and Omega of your existence and all life, enables you to triumph!